BTS

On June 15, 2013, a group of seven young South Korean men began their journey to superstardom. A month later, a fan base called ARMY came into being and spread across the world, faithfully following the lives and work of RM, Jin, J-Hope, Jimin, Suga, V and Jung Kook.

ARMY's devotion to the BangTanSonyeondan, later shortened to BTS, propelled the talented singers and dancers out of their native country and onto the global stage. Thanks to active social media and fan-provided translations of lyrics and YouTube videos, people in many other countries began to appreciate the Bangtan Boys. Their songs spoke to a generation – all about the struggles of youth, maintaining your mental health, having self-esteem and making the most of yourself even when it seems the world is against you.

They were role models for caring for others, respecting your family, working hard and never giving up on yourself.

They formed a strong bond with their fans, acknowledging the love and support and what it meant to them and their success, by holding live online sessions and in-person meets.

Then, after nine years of love and excitement, growing audiences and rocketing album sales and livestreams, came the shock announcement: the group would be taking a break while they fulfilled their national obligation to do military service. They would also take time out to pursue solo projects and experiment with their personal styles before bringing their experiences back to the group.

ARMY has had to be very patient, keeping up their spirits with occasional song releases and supporting those members on their individual journeys. But now that's all in the past – the boys have returned to the group and BTS is raring to go, with a new album and a world tour in the offing.

In this publication we look back at the boys' careers so far and forward to the future, to understand what makes them so special and why 2026 is going to be a great year!

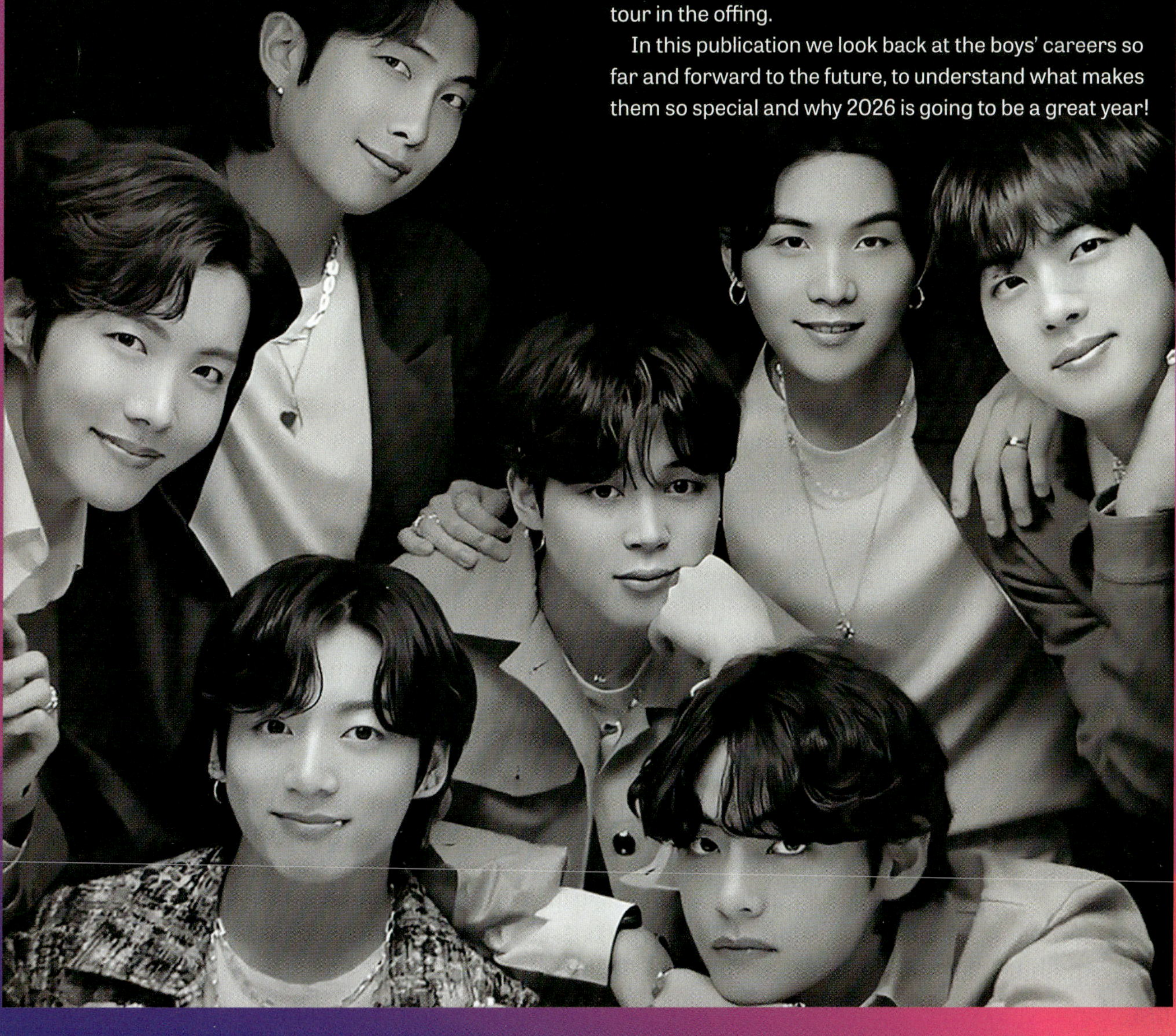

Mischief Managed BTS, CC BY 4.0 via Wikimedia Commons

Kimberly Chanhpheng/dreamstime.com

Contents

10 Seconds, CC BY 4.0 via Wikimedia Commons

The White House, Public domain via Wikimedia Commons

Bangtan Blog, CC BY 4.0 via Wikimedia Commons

Page 105
WIN
$250 AMAZON VOUCHER TO SPLASH ON BTS MERCH OF YOUR CHOICE

Public domain

DARE U JK, CC BY 3.0 via Wikimedia Commons

BTS giving their debut performance in Seoul on June 15, 2013.

Welcome The Return!

The Bangtan Boys are back! A break to pursue solo projects and do their military service duty has taken BTS away from ARMY for far too long. Now they are full-on working towards their next album and global tour in 2026, and we couldn't be happier.

How It All Began

2005 Music producer and songwriter Bang Si-hyuk forms Big Hit Entertainment company.

2010 Bang signs 15-year-old Kim Nam-joon (RM), intending to create a hip-hop group but instead decides to form an idol group with RM as the leader.

2010 Auditions are held for BangTanSonyeondan (translation: Bulletproof Boy Scouts) and Jin, Suga, Jimin, V, J-Hope and Jung Kook come on board as trainees.

2011 Intensive vocal coaching, dance training and music writing for the trainees as they transform themselves into a close-knit team. BangTanSonyeondan becomes BTS, aka Bangtan Boys.

2012 BTS stage their first performance for music industry insiders – their debut is planned for 2013.

2013 In June the debut single *No More Dream* is released and the road to superstardom begins.

2013 A month after BTS makes their debut, their official fan club is formed. It takes the name ARMY, which stands for Adorable Representative M C for Youth.

David Becker/Getty Images

The Las Vegas Strip lights up for the BTS shows in April 2022.

The Importance Of Purple

The world will light up in purple when the Bangtan Boys embark on their comeback tour in 2026!

It was V who came up with "borahae", meaning "I purple you". It's a sort of clever play on the Korean for I love you – saranghae – coupled with the Korean for purple, which is bora.

As V explained, because the colour purple is the final colour of a rainbow, so borahae means to love and trust for a long time. He meant it to be a symbol of the strong bond between BTS and ARMY but it has become much more than that.

"I Purple You" was used by UNICEF in 2021 in its global anti-bullying campaign. On their previous tours, cities have lit up their famous landmarks with a purple glow, and when BTS performed the *Permission To Dance On Stage* concerts in Las Vegas in 2022, even the famous Las Vegas Strip turned purple in a Viva Borahaegas way.

So look out world! Borahae is on its way!

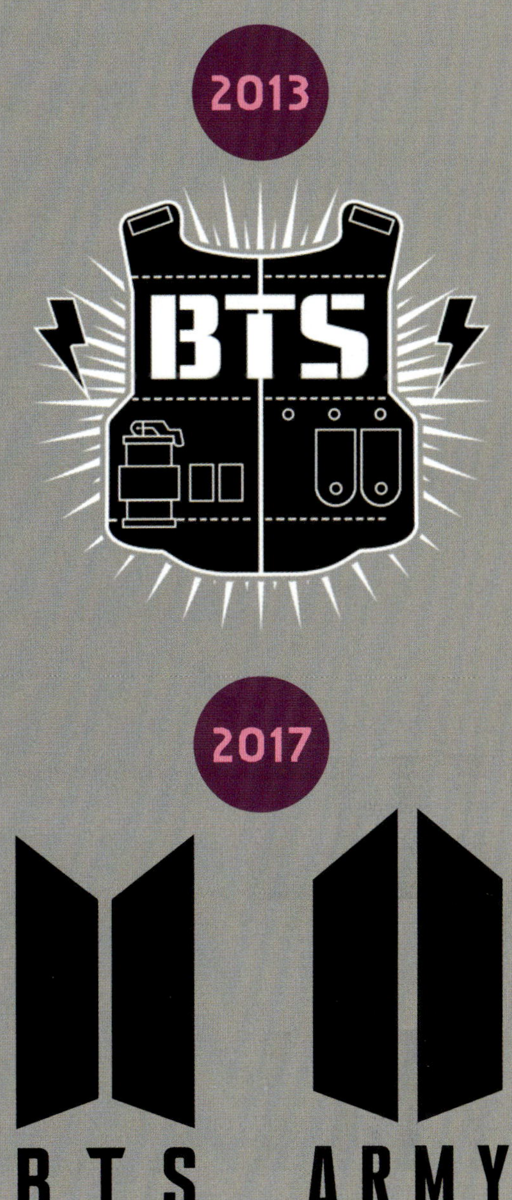

The BTS Logo

The 2013 debut logo reflected the Bulletproof Boy Scouts, with the flak jacket symbolising the BTS mission to protect young people from prejudice, unjust criticism and unrealistic expectations.

In 2017 the logo changed to a pair of half-open doors seen from the inside, which represent BTS opening new doors on the world. The meaning of BTS changed at the same time to Beyond The Scene to match the visual.

Following on, ARMY adopted a logo of the same doors seen from the outside, which represent the fans waiting to receive BTS. Put one on top of the other they form a shield, demonstrating that the boys and the fans are always there to protect each other.

Timeline to Success

June 2013
Debut album *2 Cool 4 Skool*

February 2014
Skool Luv Affair release

July 2014
First US concert - *Show & Prove*

August 2014
Dark & Wild album release

October 2014
Start of *Red Bullet Tour*

February 2015
Wake Up: Open Your Eyes Japan tour

April 2015
The Most Beautiful Moment in Life
EP release

November 2015
*The Most Beautiful Moment in Life,
Part 2* release

November 2015
The Most Beautiful Moment in Life
Asia tour

May 2016
*The Most Beautiful Moment in Life:
Young Forever* release

October 2016
Wings album release

November 2016
Young Forever Melon Music Awards'
Album of the Year

Showcasing the *Dark & Wild* album in Seoul on August 19, 2014.

The Chosunilbo JNS/Getty Images

**Receiving the prestigious Melon Music
Award for Best Dance at the Olympic
Park, Seoul, on November 7, 2015.**

Meet BT21!

In 2017 BTS came up with the idea of having cartoon friends for each of the group members that would reflect their characters. The boys drew sketches of what they wanted their friend to look like and described their personalities.

The friends are Koya (for RM), RJ (for Jin), Shooky (for Suga), Mang (for J-Hope), Chimmy (for Jimin), Tata (for V), Cooky (for Jung Kook), and an eighth, Van, who was created to represent ARMY.

Timeline to Success

February 2017
Wings tour to Asia, Americas and Oceania

September 2017
Love Yourself: Her album release

October 2017
UNICEF Korea/BTS *Love Myself* campaign

April 2018
Face Yourself album release

May 2018
Love Yourself: Tear album release

August 2018
Love Yourself: Answer album release with *Idol* video

August 2018
Love Yourself World Tour of Asia, Europe and Americas

September 2018
At UN General Assembly for *Generation Unlimited* campaign

April 2019
Map of the Soul: Persona release

January 2020
BTS perform at the Grammy Awards

February 2020
Map of the Soul: 7 album release

June 2020
Virtual concert *Bang Bang Con: The Live*

Matt Winkelmeyer/Getty Images

Winning three categories at the American Music Awards 2021 – Artist of the Year, Favorite Duo or Group and Favorite Pop Song for *Butter*.

Timeline to Success

August 2020
Dynamite first English single release

October 2020
Virtual *Map of the Soul: ON:E*, broadcast for ARMY

November 2020
Be release (featuring *Dynamite*)

May 2021
Butter single release

July 2021
Permission to Dance release

September 2021
My Universe (with Coldplay) release

October 2021
Permission to Dance On Stage in Seoul, LA & Las Vegas

June 2022
Proof anthology release

June 2022
Pause announced for military service and solos

June 2025
Military service completed by all members

June 2025
New 2026 album and world tour announced

July 2025
Permission to Dance On Stage – Live album release

Fact!

The World Of BTS

At birth, you're one year old, and you're a year older at New Year, not on your birthday. So if you were born on December 31 you are two years old the very next day!

To be in tune with our seven idols it's good to understand a bit about South Korea. Being born there has shaped them to be the fabulous people they are and here's a few reasons why.

South Korea has become so cool since K-pop and K-drama began to be appreciated abroad. Rightly so! BTS and other Korean groups, actors and producers have shown how much artistic talent there is in the country, and not just in music and film.

The unique Korean culture and traditions are at the heart of everything, so let's start with a little bit of history and some information on how to be on your best behaviour in South Korea.

How South Korea Came About

In ancient times the Korean peninsula was divided into lots of different kingdoms and the people into clans. These ancestral ties are still important in Korean society and the members of BTS, apart from Junk Kook, have a family clan. Even without a clan, time-honoured family rules still apply and BTS follow those traditions – respect for your elders, knowing your place with family, friends and co-workers, and caring for others.

In modern times Korea was occupied by Japan but at the end of World War Two, the country was split in two. One side, the north, became allied to the communist Soviet Union and China, the other, the south, to the democratic West.

The new North Korean government, though, believed it was the rightful ruler of the whole of Korea and invaded South Korea in 1950. The world's superpowers joined in and there was fierce fighting in which one million military personnel and up to three million civilians died. The conflict ended in 1953 with the country still divided and North Korea closing its borders to outsiders. This bloody history and the bravery of the Korean people is something BTS has written about in some of their songs.

It's common to cover your mouth when you smile or laugh.

Sniffing is more acceptable in public than blowing your nose.

The number 4 is very unlucky – when spoken it sounds like the word for death.

Behaving Well

Korean society was built on the teaching of the Chinese philosopher, Confucius. This emphasises the importance of education, studying, memorising and passing exams. The motto of the Korean education system is 'Hongik Ingan' – to live for the greater benefit of all humanity. This means not doing things for personal gain but in a way that supports others and contributes to the wellbeing of society, and it's clear that's what BTS strives to do.

Family is regarded as more important than the individual and you are bound to show respect for your living family as well as your ancestors. It has been essential for the happiness of everyone in BTS to have the support and approval of their parents – while they were trainees and even now in their successful careers.

The workplace is viewed as an extension of the family, which shows in the relationships the group has with the managers and producers at Big Hit Entertainment. You will often hear a member of BTS saying the most important thing is the team and being part of it, even while they are forging their solo careers.

BTS demonstrating almost every kind of 'aegyo' gesture you can make at one of their fan days in 2013.

Getting to Know BTS

Now a few lessons in being a bit more like BTS and understanding where they're coming from.

You won't hear any of the members of BTS being seriously rude to each other – they might have a joke or pull a prank, but they are never unkind. If they're angry or upset they hide it, putting harmony in the group above everything. Being rude would result in losing face and making everyone else feel uncomfortable.

The same goes for ARMY. BTS cherish their fans and all members go out of their way to acknowledge how important their beloved ARMYs are to them. Ignoring or dismissing them would reflect very badly and would disturb the whole group.

Koreans also go out of their way to avoid embarrassing other people, as well as themselves. The BTS boys can often be seen on Weverse and at ARMY meets smoothing over awkward situations and making sure there are no hurt feelings or damaged pride.

People bow to each other all the time when they meet to show their respect, and you will notice BTS members bowing to their audience, in person or on screen, at the beginning of every encounter. This must be done with heads down, eyes closed and hands clasped together,

Fact!

Everything is given and received with two hands – tickets, food, gifts, pouring drinks, handshakes. You'll see BTS wave with both hands to show their fans respect.

Group IDD, CC BY-SA 3.0 via Wikimedia Commons

Fact!

Kimchi (pickled vegetables) are so important there's a museum in Seoul dedicated to their history and preparation.

Fact!

You won't see anyone in BTS writing a name in red ink – that colour's reserved for someone who's dead.

Fact!

Cooking and sharing a meal, eating from the same bowls and not having your own plate are a feature of Korean culture.

Fact!

Being affectionate in public is frowned on, so couples proclaim their love by wearing matching clothing.

The Importance of Being Polite

WHAT IS AEGYO?

Fans of K-pop and K-drama will be very familiar with people showing aegyo or being described as having a lot of aegyo. It means cuteness and it's used to show affection and closeness. It's mostly practised by girls, but it's not unknown for male idols to do a bit of aegyo, too.

There are lots of ways of showing aegyo: acting playful, using a high-pitched, child-like voice, looking upwards and sideways as you talk, winking and using your hands continuously – clasping them under your chin or at the top of your chest, making V signs and jazz hands, pointing at your lips, your eyes, your cheeks or the side of your head, tracing the shape of your face, and saluting.

You also make a lot of heart shapes – with both hands in front of you, with fingers crossed above a fist (tiny heart sign) and with a hand cupped on the side of your face (cheek heart).

Words to know

Korean is a hierarchical language, this means that age and rank are important. When you meet someone for the first time it's common to ask their age so you know how to address them.

Oppa – older brother, endearment only used by girls/women to address an older male friend, family member or boyfriend. ARMYs will use this if they are younger than their idol.

Hyong – older brother, used by boys/men when talking about an older male friend or a brother. Jung Kook will use this when talking to other members of BTS because he is the youngest.

Onni – older sister, used by females to address an older woman friend or family member.

Nuna – older sister, used by males with an older friend or sister. BTS might refer to someone in ARMY who is older than them as nuna.

Sonbae – senior, used at school or at work with anyone who is a higher rank or more experienced.

Hubae – junior, for anyone at work or school who is below you in position or class.

KIM NAM-JOON

김남준

All About RM

Real name:
Kim Nam-joon

Nicknames:
Runch Randa, Dance Prodigy, Rap Monster, RapMon, RM, God of Destruction

ARMY call him:
Namjoon, Joon or Joonie

Born:
September 12, 1994 in Sangdo-dong, an area in the Dongjak district of Seoul.

Grew up:
in Ilsan District in the city of Goyang, a suburb of Seoul where his family moved when he was around four years old.

Family:
his dad, Kim Beom, is a businessman and his mum works in real estate. His sister, Kim Kyung Min, is three years his junior.

Clan:
Gangneung Kim, descendants of Kim Chuwon, who was Prince of Myŏngju, modern-day Gangneung on the northeast coast of South Korea.

Han Myung-Gu/Getty Images

“**One of the region's most dexterous rappers, capable of switching flows effortlessly as he glides across an array of diverse instrumentals.**”
Peter A Berry, journalist and culture critic

Languages:
Korean, Japanese, English

Height:
181cm (5ft 11in)

Position in BTS:
leader, main rapper, lyric writer

Vocal range:
baritone

Instruments:
piano, guitar, saxophone

Currently living:
Yongsan-gu district of Seoul in an apartment in the Hannam The Hill complex.

The Chosunilbo JNS/Getty Images

“**Life is perhaps not about finding shining moments among the worthless, but realising that what had seemed worthless were really the shining moments.**”
RM

Social media:
www.instagram.com/rkive/
www.instagram.com/rpwprpwprpwp/

Inside & Outside RM

Korea Dispatch, CC BY 3.0 via Wikimedia

Military service: December 2023 – June 2025
Rank of private; played saxophone in the military band

Endorsement and brand ambassador: K'hawah Coffee (2015), Seoul Tourism (2022), Bottega Veneta high-end Italian men's clothing line (2023), Iloom (2023), Samsung (2023-24), Samsung Art TV (2025)

Hobbies: collecting Korean art, visiting museums, cycling, reading (everything! - novels, poetry, philosophy, history and art books), photography, growing bonsai trees

Pets: American Eskimo dog called Rapmon, aka Moni, that sadly died in 2023 just before RM enlisted

BT21 character:
Koya, a multi-talented blue koala who's very sleepy but with a mind full of thoughts.

Fav colour: black

BTS 7 tattoo: on his ankle

Health: Operation in 2018 to straighten the partition inside his nose between the two nasal cavities.

Favourite foods: Korean knife noodles (Kalgukso), Jajangmyeon noodles in black bean sauce, Paldo Bibimyeon spicy cold noodles, BBQ pork belly, watermelon

Favourite things: Ryan the maneless lion from the Kakao Friends product range, growing plants, comfortable street wear, hats and accessories

Bad habits: breaking things, talking to himself, losing things, borrowing other people's things and not returning them

Ideal girl: tall, pale, sexy, confident, nice voice

Childhood dreams: to be a superhero and save the world, or a security guard in an apartment block

Personal style: cool vibes, classy, smart, minimalistic elegance

Mischief Managed BTS, CC BY 4.0 via Wikimedia Commons

Performing at the Mnet Asian Music Awards on December 3, 2014.

What!
He can't blow bubblegum bubbles

"There's no way to understand things so easily and so deeply as with books."

What!
He is good at ice skating

On the day of his discharge from compulsory military service, June 10, 2025.

The Chosunilbo JNS/Getty Images

RM is Super Smart!

- Taught himself English by watching TV, especially the sitcom *Friends*

- Graduated from Apgujeong High School in 2013

- Has an IQ of 148

- Was in the top 1% in Korean university entrance exams for Maths, Languages, Social Studies

- Studied Broadcasting & Entertainment at Global Cyber University between 2014 and 2019

- Enrolled for Master of Business Administration in Advertising & Media at Hanyang Cyber University in March 2019 and is continuing studies

"Strangely, everything I touch breaks. The legs of my sunglasses snap off, or the refrigerator handle falls off."

Work outside music

Bangtan Blog, CC BY 4.0 via Wikimedia

- Played himself in *4things Show – Rap Monster* a documentary

- Regular on variety TV programme *Problematic Man* in 2015 as one of the "men with hot brains". He had to solve puzzles and problems by discussing his thoughts and sharing experiences with other panellists

- Host on a variety of TV programmes – Inkigayo music show, *M Countdown* and *The Dictionary of Useless Knowledge* – in 2016, 2017 and 2022

- Has made three addresses at United Nations events:
  2018 Generation Unlimited conference to tackle global education and training
  2020 presentation at the 75th General Assembly to deliver a message of hope to young people during the Covid-19 pandemic
  2021 address about challenges of the pandemic, poverty, youth and climate change

- In 2023, appointed Public Relations Ambassador for the Ministry of National Defence Agency's team that aims to find and identify remains of the fallen from the Korean War

- Gave a talk at Art Basel (that promotes contemporary art) in Switzerland in June 2025

Performing as Rap Monster with BTS in July 2015.

Toomuch940912, CC BY 4.0 via Wikimedia Commons

What! Has written 230 songs, and counting…

Promoting the release of Butter on May 21, 2021.

The Chosunilbo JNS/Getty Images

RM's Music

Influences: hip-hop's Epik High, rapper Eminem, Zico (later leader of Block B band), UK electropop duo Honne, Kanye West, A$AP Rocky

Pre-training: Rapping in hip-hop clubs at 13 and joined rap crew Daenamhyup
First concert at 14

Auditions: Big Deal Records in 2009 – failed because he forgot some lyrics in the second round of interviews. Rapper and reality TV star Sleepy is a judge at the audition and tells Big Hit Entertainment producer Pdogg about him.
Invited to audition for Big Hit Entertainment CEO Bang Si-hyuk in 2010 – succeeded and became a trainee from 2010 to 2013.

First solo: August 2014 *What am I to You?* Intro rap track on BTS studio album *Dark & Wild*

First solo mixtape: *RM* in March 2015

Second solo mixtape: *mono* in October 2018

Solo singles: *Persona* in March 2019

First solo studio album: *Indigo* in December 2022

Second solo studio album: *Right Place, Wrong Person* in May 2024

Film documentary: *RM: Right People, Wrong Place* – about the eight months leading up to his military service. Premiered at the Busan International Film Festival in October 2024 and globally in December 2024.

"In 2011 I made a song by myself and at the very end of the song there was a part when I had to yell out 'Rap Monster'. I don't know if that part was memorable or not, but the Company staff started calling me that and it eventually became my name."

What! Introduced to Eminem's music by his schoolteacher at age 11

"Even if you're not perfect you're a limited edition."

Waiting to perform at the 64th Annual Grammy Awards in Las Vegas on April 3, 2022.

Sharing the love... and the money

2019	$72,000 to help Korean hearing-impaired students to get a musical education
2020	$72,000 to print and distribute rare art books to rural schools and libraries
2021 to date	$72,000 given every year to help in restoring and preserving Korean cultural artifacts being exhibited overseas
2022	$72,000 printing an art brochure to introduce Korean paintings
2023	$72,000 to develop forensic science in Korea
2024	$72,000 for providing welfare and medical treatment for former service personnel and the families of those who died in service of their country
2025	$72,000 for relief efforts following wildfires in three Korean regions

Korean currency is the won. The 2025 currency rates are used in this book to convert the donations BTS have made to dollars.

All About Jin

KIM SEOK-JIN

김석진

On the day he left military service after 18 months.

Real name:
Kim Seok-jin

Nicknames:
Worldwide Handsome, Mom of the Group, Pink Princess

ARMY call him:
Seokjin, Jinnie, Eomma

Born:
December 4, 1992 in Anyang, Gyeonggi Province, south of Seoul

Grew up:
Gwacheon, Gyeonggi-do Province where his family moved when he was a baby

Family:
Dad is CEO of a company that supplies parts to Samsung. He and Jin used to do charity work together. Mum is a homemaker and brother, Kim Seokjung, is two years older.

Clan:
Gwangsan Kim, descendants of the third son of King Sinmu in the 9th century Korean kingdom of Silla. The same clan as V's family.

Languages:
Korean, some English, some Japanese

> **"Because so many people love seeing me on stage and because I can make many people happy, I become happy through them."**
> Jin

Height:
178cm (5ft 10in)

Position in BTS:
vocalist and visuals

Vocal range:
tenor, can sing falsetto

Instruments:
piano and guitar

Currently living:
Yongsan-gu district of Seoul in an apartment in the Hannam The Hill complex. He is a neighbour of RM.

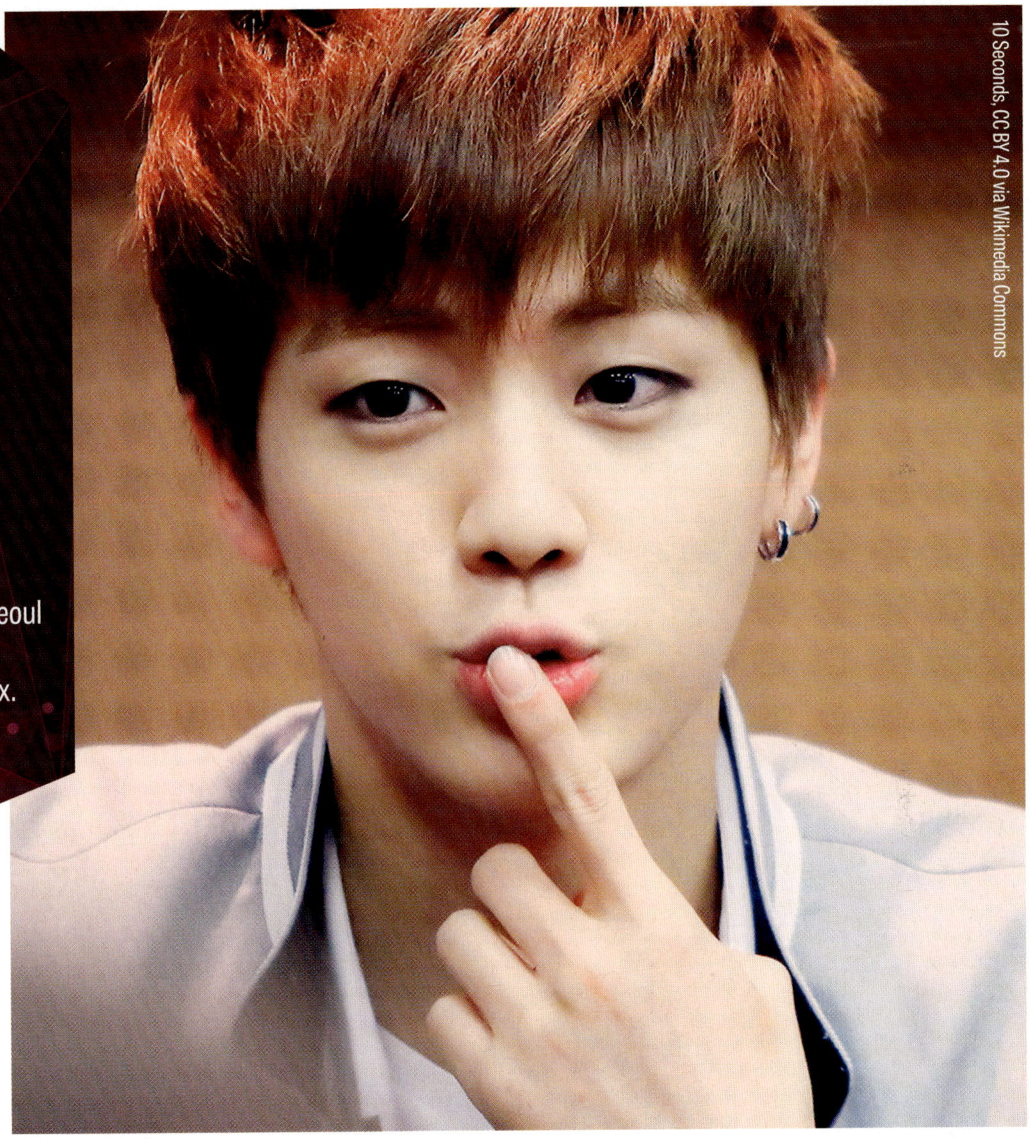

> **"When we're with strangers, if Jin hyung says light jokes, the mood lights up really well. He's really good with ice-breaking."**
> Fellow band member RM

Social media:
www.instagram.com/jin/
www.instagram.com/jin_bighitentertainment/

Inside & Outside Jin

Military service: December 2022 to June 2024. Appointed Assistant Training Instructor

Education:
Bosung High School graduate in 2011
Konkuk University degree in Film & Visual Arts in 2017
Hanyang Cyber University to study for a master's degree in Film

Endorsement and brand ambassador: Gucci fashions (2024-date), Laneige skincare (2024-date), Fred Jewelry (2024-date), Alo clothing (2024-date), Jin Ramen by Otoki (2022 and 2025) and Visit Seoul (2024-date)

Hobbies: cooking, playing video games, snowboarding, tennis, golf, collecting Mario & MapleStory merch

Pets: until 2019 he had two sugar gliders, Eomuk and Odeng (both mean Fishcake but Odeng is Japanese). He now has one called Gukmul (Soup)

BT21 character: RJ, a kind and compassionate white alpaca who loves cooking, eating and making people feel at home.

Fav colour: pink

BTS 7 tattoo: above his waist on the left side

Health: underwent surgery in 2022 to repair a tendon in his left index finger after it was damaged while he was exercising

Favourite foods: strawberries, lobster, crunchy Korean fried chicken with a sweet-spicy sauce, naengmyeon cold noodles

Favourite things: food, animated films, sleeping, blowing kisses to ARMY

Dislikes: bugs crawling on him, scary horror movies

Bad habits: sitting with bad posture, getting totally wrapped up in video games, imagining he has all sorts of bad illnesses

Ideal girl: good cook, kind, caring

Childhood dreams: to be a detective, then a journalist and finally an actor

Personal style: style icon, elegant with natural charisma and modern flair, full of positive energy

What! Can open a bag of potato snacks with his toes

Performing at the Culture and Arts Festival in Seoul on October 13, 2013.

Carrying the Olympic torch for South Korea in Paris on July 14, 2024.

Jin the Big Brother

Even more than the rest of the band, Jin is caring and protective of the group, cooking for them and raising their spirits if they are down. He's always ready with a cheesy joke and a positive vibe. As V has said, "He might have a weaker inner side, but what he shows to us members is very strong and [he] takes care of us one by one."

Although he is the eldest of the seven, the others often refer to him at the 'maknae', the youngest in a family group, because he has such a youthful attitude and his face never seems to age.

Throughout its history, Jin has been the glue that holds BTS together. J-Hope summed it up when he said: "I think he plays the most important role of maintaining the team together. I think he gives us strength."

"Worries. Everyone has worries. You might feel a little unhappy when you have them, but it will pass, and soon after you'll feel happiness again."

What!

He co-owns a Japanese-style restaurant, Ossu Seiromushi, with his brother

Work outside music

- In 2015 began the live stream *Eat Jin* on the BTS V Live channel, a mukbang show which involves eating large quantities of food while answering ARMY questions.

- He has joined in two addresses at United Nations events delivering hope during the pandemic and facing the challenges of modern life.

- Carried the Olympic torch in the 2022 relay in Paris.

- Opened the first Ossu Seiromushi restaurant in Songpagu District, Seoul, with his brother in 2018, serving thinly sliced and steamed meat, vegetables and seafood. This closed in 2020 but was replaced by a new restaurant in Yeongdeungpo-gu district.

- Co-founded Jini's Lamp Agricultural Corporation in 2024, with a well-known Korean TV chef, Baek Jong-won. The company manufactures IGIN alcoholic drinks made from fermented rice, apples, watermelons and plums.

- Star of web series *Run Jin* where he tackles games and challenges.

- Participant on variety, reality and talk shows in Korea and Japan such as *Half Star Hotel in Lost Island*, *Handsome Guys*, *Since Those Days* and *Salon Drip*.

On top of the Empire State Building in New York in May 2025.

What! He was named 'world's most handsome face' in a poll, beating 18,000 people from 58 countries

Jin's Music

Influences: Chris Martin from Coldplay, Michael Jackson in the 80s and 90s for dancing, his fellow BTS members for songwriting, 90s Korean pop music for his vocal style

Pre-training: Approached by a scout from K-pop agency SM Entertainment while in High School, but turned them down, thinking the offer was a hoax.

Auditions: Invited to audition by Big Hit Entertainment in 2011 when a scout saw him getting off a bus. Auditioned as an actor but as a result he won a spot as a BTS trainee. As he had no experience in singing or dancing, his class work was intense to get to the same level as fellow band members.

First solo song: *Awake* on the *Wings* album

First solo release: *Tonight* for the 2019 BTS Festa

Second solo release: *Abyss* in 2020

Third solo release: *Super Tuna* in 2021

First solo collaboration: *The Astronaut* with British rock band Coldplay in 2022

First solo studio album: *Happy* in November 2024

Second solo studio album: *Echo* in May 2025

"If there is something lacking when we're doing our job, he works hard to fill that lacking part... he works hard silently for our team and that is very touching..." Fellow band member Jimin

Worldwide Handsome spreading some love for the *Butter* single in 2021.

What!
Once said he would date Suga – but only if he was a girl

Sharing the love... and the money

2018 to date	monthly donations to UNICEF Korea; became a member of its Honors Club in 2019 for donating more than $72,000 in a year; total given to date is more than $245,000
2018	food, blankets and bowls to Korean animal rights and welfare organisations
2021	food for the Beagle Rescue Network of Korea that rescues dogs used in laboratory experiments
2025	$72,000 to the Korea University Medical Center to help terminally ill patients in developing countries

MIN YOON-GI

민윤기

Performing on *The Red Bullet* tour in Seoul in October 2014.

Marshmallow, CC BY 4.0 via Wikimedia Commons

Real name:
Min Yoon-gi

Nicknames:
Agust D, D-Boy, Min PD, Min Snail

ARMY call him:
Yoongi, Shookga (when he suddenly gets active), Gloss (the meaning of the name Yoon-gi in English)

Born:
March 9, 1993 in Daegu, North Gyeongsang Province in southeast Korea

Family:
Dad is a businessman, mum runs her own restaurant and he has an older brother, Jun Ki

Clan:
Yeoheung Min, descendants of Min Ching-do, a Chinese emissary who settled in the Korean state of Goryeo in the 10th century

Languages:
Korean, reasonable English, basic Japanese

Height:
174cm (5ft 7in)

"In general, what fans talk about and think about become very important sources of inspiration to us, because we want to write something that's real to people..."

Position in BTS:
vocalist, lyric writer

Work as Agust D:
rapper, producer, songwriter

Vocal range:
baritone

Instruments:
piano

Currently living:
the UN Village in Hannam-dong with a view of the Han River, with bright coloured walls, modern furniture and an impressive collection of bottles of spirits

Marie Claire Korea, CC BY 3.0 via Wikimedia Commons

"Those who don't have a dream, it's okay. It's okay if you don't have a dream. You just have to be happy."

Social media:
www.instagram.com/agustd/
www.instagram.com/suga_bighitentertainment/

Inside & Outside Suga

On the red carpet for the Billboard Music Awards in 2019.

Dispatch, CC BY 3.0 via Wikimedia Commons

Military service: September 2023 to June 2025, given position as a social worker

Education:
Graduated from Apgujeong High School in 2011 and Korea Arts School in 2012
Gained a degree in Broadcasting and Entertainment from the Global Cyber University in 2019
Enrolled in Hanyang Cyber University to study for a Masters of Business Administration in Advertising and Media

Endorsement and brand ambassador: Seoul Tourism (2022), Valentino fashion (2023), National Basketball Association (2023-24), Samsung (2023-24)

Hobbies: fixing things, interior design, basketball, cooking, reading comics, photography

Pets: toy poodle called Holly that belongs to his parents

Fav colour: white

BT21 character:
Shooky, a mischievous brown cookie who hates milk but loves playing pranks on friends.

BTS 7 tattoo: on his left shoulder

Health: appendicitis in 2013, fell and suffered an ear injury in 2016, had to have surgery on the cartilage in his shoulder in 2020, has suffered on and off from depression and social anxiety

Favourite foods: skewered lamb, kimchi stew, medium-rare steak

Favourite things: sleeping whenever he gets the chance, quiet places, Japanese mascot Kumamon because it looks stupid

Dislikes: crowds and noise

Bad habits: biting his nails

In trouble: sentenced to a fine of 15 million Won ($13,112) in September 2024 for driving an electric scooter under the influence of alcohol

Ideal girl: similar in taste to himself, calm, wise, likes music

Childhood dreams: to be a firefighter, a professional basketball player and a musician

Personal style: can come across as cold and aloof but is actually warm inside

What!

The name Suga comes from the first syllables of 'shooting guard' – shoo ga – his student basketball position

"I try not to be influenced by success or popularity."

Behind the scenes during the 2020 filming of Suga's music video *Daechwita*, performed in the person of his alter ego Agust D.

What!

Gets called Minstradamus because his predictions often come true

Work outside music

- 2022 talk show web series on YouTube called *Suchwita* where Suga interviews guests over drinks.

- He has joined in with the rest of BTS in two addresses at United Nations events

- 2023 made documentary *Suga: Road to D-Day* about a musical trip around the world to find inspiration for his songs.

> "I always enjoy meeting and talking to musicians. I enjoy meeting people. We may speak different languages, but we share the same mind."

Appearing on *The Today Show* in the US on February 21, 2020.

Suga's Alter Ego

Running alongside his work as a member of BTS, Suga has been building his career as a hardcore rapper under the name Agust D. This sprang from his early days as an underground rapper, before he joined Bit Hit Entertainment as a trainee.

Yoon-gi's birth city, Daegu, had a notable underground music scene that inspired the young boy to compose and produce. He and his fellow artists left mainstream hip-hop in favour of new, hard-hitting music.

Eventually, Yoon-gi moved to Seoul, despite his parent's objections, where Suga was born and joined BTS while his alter ego, Agust D, carved a niche as a tougher star, working from his own studio, the Genius Lab.

Suga's Music

Influences: rappers Stony Skunk, Epik High, Kanye West, Lupe Fiasco, Lil Wayne, Hit Boy, Eminem

Pre-training: Began as a rapper called Gloss while he was in High School and produced, composed and performed with his hometown artists D-Town in 2010.

Auditions: Saw a flyer for a rap competition run by Big Hit Entertainment, entered and got second place and a signing as a trainee and producer.

Song writing: created his studio as a creative space and called it the Genius Lab

First solo song: *First Love* on the *Wings* album in 2016

First solo mixtape: *Agust D* in 2016

Second solo mixtape: *D-2* in 2020

First solo album (as Agust D): *D-Day* in 2023

First solo world tour: the *D-Day* tour in 2023, visiting the US, Indonesia, Thailand, Singapore, Japan and, of course, South Korea

" I want my music to become that light for those in the dark. I want them to heal from it and find the courage to step forward again."

Steven Ferdman/Getty Images

Good Causes

2018	donated beef to 39 Korean orphanages in the name of ARMY, as he had promised his fans he would buy them meat if he succeeded as an artist
2019	$82,000 and 329 BT21 Shooky dolls to the Korean Pediatric Cancer Foundation
2020	$72,000 to the Hope Bridge National Disaster Relief Association to combat Covid-19 in his home town, Daegu
2021	$72,000 to Daegu's Keimyung Hospital to fund underprivileged children with cancer
2022	$72,000 to Hope Bridge National Disaster Relief Association to help victims of wildfires on Korea's east coast
2023	$72,000 to Korean Save the Children to buy bedding and school supplies for children affected by the earthquake in southern Turkey and northern Syria
2025	$72,000 to the Korean Red Cross for wildfire relief
2025	$4 million to the Severance Hospital in Sinchon-dong, Seodaemun District of Seoul to build a centre for children with autism

JUNG HO-SEOK

정호석

Performing at the 2018 Melon Music Awards in Seoul.

HopeSmiling, CC BY 4.0 via Wikimedia Commons

All About J-Hope

Real name:
Jung Ho-seok

Nicknames:
J-Hope, J-Dope, J-Horse, Cheonsa (Angel)

ARMY call him:
Hobi

Born:
February 18, 1994 in Gwangju in Korea's southwest

Family:
Mum and dad, a teacher. Older sister by four years, Jung Jiwoo, aka Mejiwoo, a model, influencer and CEO of fashion label AJ Look, Fun the Mental spectacles, skincare brand neaf neaf

Clan:
Hadong Jeong, descendants of Jeong Son-wi, who served in the 11th century government of King Sukjong of Goryeo (until 1392 the name of the whole of the Korean peninsula)

Languages:
Korean, Chinese

Height:
177cm (5ft 10in)

"When things get tough, look at the people who love you! You will get energy from them."
J-Hope

Position in BTS:
vocalist, choreographer

Vocal range:
tenor

Instruments:
recorder (including playing it with his nose!)

Currently living:
in a luxury apartment in the Forest Trimage complex in Seoul and a house in Gwangju, with a spiral staircase and a large Hope World mural in the garden

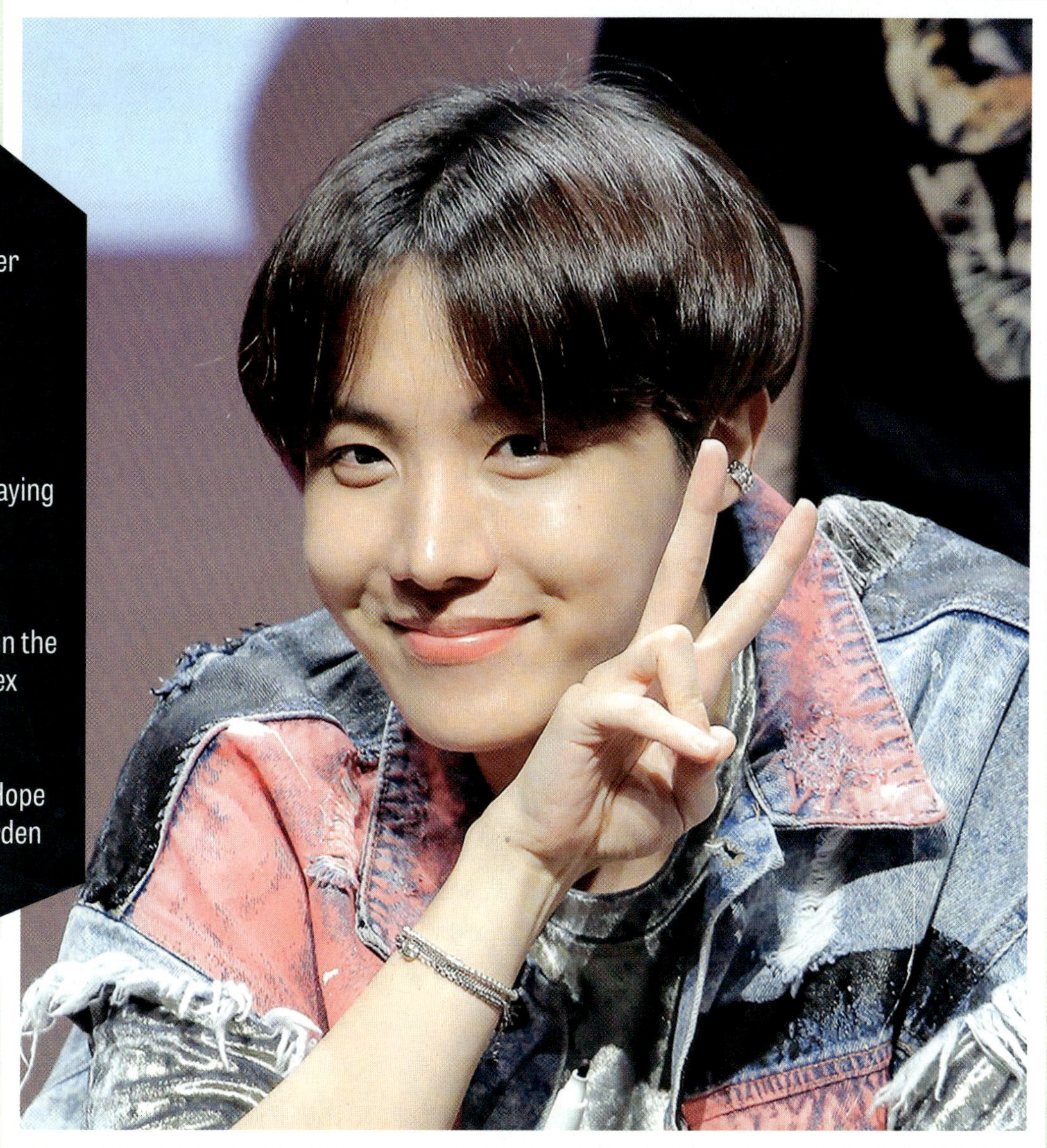

"Although J-Hope is a world star now, he doesn't let fame distract him. He's still as humble and polite as ever. He still asks for advice from those around him, and he's always respectful when speaking to people, even in phone calls."
Park Daehong, CEO of Joy Dance Academy where J-Hope studied

Social media:
www.instagram.com/uarmyhope/
www.instagram.com/jhope_bighitentertainment/

www.tiktok.com/@iamurhope

Going into rehearsals for an appearance on Korean entertainment TV programme *Music Bank* in 2022.

The Chosunilbo JNS/Getty Images

Inside & Outside J-Hope

Military service: April 2023 to October 2024, appointed as an Assistant Training Instructor

Education:
Dance classes at Gwangju Music Academy, winning local prizes

Endorsement and brand ambassador: Samsung (2023), Louis Vuitton fashion house (2023 and 2025-date)

Hobbies: listening to music, window shopping, collecting Brick Bear models and Kaws, Kermit and Peanuts soft toys

Pets: a brown and white Shih Tzu called Mickey that belonged to his parents

Fav colour: green

BTS 7 tattoo: above his Achilles tendon on his right leg

Health: suffered from a fever while on tour with the band in May 2025 in Mexico

Favourite foods: kimchi, Sprite, bulgogi (Korean BBQ meat), fried chicken, tiramisu

Favourite things: the sea, reading, someone stroking his hair

Dislikes: the nickname J-Horse, working out

Bad habits: messy eating

Ideal girl: likes books, is caring, a good cook, feminine

BT21 character: dancing machine Mang, a purple character who wears a blue horse mask so you can only see his heart-shaped smile when he takes it off.

Childhood dreams: to fly in an airplane, to become a dancer

Personal style: upbeat and energetic

What!
J-Hope won a national dance championship in 2008, when he was 14

"I remember being captivated by Jules Verne's *Twenty Thousand Leagues Under the Seas* when I read it as a kid."

Watching a basketball game between the Los Angeles Lakers and the Golden State Warriors in 2025.

Michael Owens/Getty Images

> "I feel like I live with a sense of mission. Rather than thinking, 'It has to be perfect!' I do what I have to do, making sure I remember the really important and fundamental things, and trust that the results will follow."

Why J-Hope nearly left BTS

The Bangtan Boys had a mentally and physically exhausting time during the early days, and the parents of some of them didn't fully agree with their choice to become trainees so they lacked family support. Big Hit Entertainment was a small company and money was tight. It wasn't clear that there would be any success for the team as a group.

Over time, J-Hope lost confidence in achieving anything significant with the group and decided he would prefer to pursue a career as a solo dance artist. When he told the boys about his decision, Jung Kook broke down in tears. His emotional reaction apparently had a profound effect on J-Hope and he began to reconsider.

Then RM, as leader of BTS, told their managing company that the group would not survive without J-Hope. "I told them that we needed Jung Ho-seok. We can't make it without him."

In the end, his faith in the talents of the other group members persuaded J-Hope to stay, they went on to debut successfully and the rest is history.

Work outside music

- He has joined in the two BTS addresses at United Nations events

- Has appeared as a guest on many talk shows and game shows in Korea and the US, such as *The Tonight Show Starring Jimmy Fallon*, *Chef & My Fridge*, *Run Jin* and *I Live Alone*

- Starred in *Inside Mang – the New Universe* in 2023, a web series now on YouTube where J-Hope's BT21 character eventually took off his horse mask to reveal his true face

- Starred in the documentary *J-Hope in the Box* about the making of his debut album in 2023

- Appeared in six-part docuseries *Hope on the Street* in 2024

Performing at the Golden Disc Awards in Seoul in 2019.

HopeSmiling, CC BY 4.0 via Wikimedia Commons

Han Myung-Gu/Getty Images

What!
If he had a superpower J-Hope says it would be to read people's minds

J-Hope's Music

Influences: rappers Kyle, Joey Badass, Aminé, A$AP Rocky, J Cole, Beenzino

Pre-training: Was a member in 2010 of an underground dance group called Neuron and his stage name was Smile Hoya

Auditions: As a dancer for JYP Entertainment in 2009, but he wasn't accepted
In 2010 the CEO of his dance academy, Park Daehong, introduced him to the Big Hit Entertainment CEO, Bang Si Hyuk, and he was taken on as a trainee

First solo release: *1 Verse* in 2015

First solo mixtape: *Hope World* in 2018

Second solo collaboration: *Chicken Noodle Soup* with US singer Becky G in 2019

First solo studio album: *Jack in the Box* in 2022

First solo performance: *Dick Clark's New Year's Rockin' Eve* from New York's Times Square in 2022

First solo tour: Hope on the Stage in February 2025, taking in major Asian and American cities

"The music helped me sympathise with our young generation and also empathise with them. I'd like to create and write more music that represents them."

Leaving day at the end of J-Hope's military service on October 17, 2024.

Helping to launch the single *Butter* with an appropriate hair colour in May 2021.

What!
He once threw a banana at Jung Kook because he was hoarding a fruit gift from ARMY

Good Causes

2018	$135,000 to Child Fund Korea to support children attending his High School in Gwangju
2019	a further $180,000 to Child Fund Korea
2020	$72,000 to children suffering the economic effects of the Covid-19 pandemic
2021	$108,000 for children with sight and hearing impairments
2021	$72,000 for children affected by violence in Tanzania in Africa
2021	$72,000 to cover heating costs for low-income families and children's medical expenses
2022	$72,000 to the Hope Bridge Korea Disaster Relief Association for flood relief in Seoul
2023	$72,000 to UNICEF Korea for emergency relief for children affected by the earthquake in southern Turkey and northern Syria
2024	$72,000 to families of the victims of the Jeju Air flight 2216 crash in December
2025	$143,000 to the Asan Medical Center Children's Hospital to improve facilities for patients and research into rare diseases
2025	$87,000 to the Hope Bridge Korea Disaster Relief Association for the effects of wildfires in three Korean regions

PARK JI-MIN

박지민

All About Jimin

Real name:
Park Ji-Min

Nicknames:
Jimin, Mo-chi

ARMY call him:
Jiminie, ChimChim

Born:
October 13, 1995 in the Geumjeong District of Busan in the southeast tip of Korea

Family:
Dad, Park Hyun-soo, and mum who run a café in Busan called Zm-millennial, and younger brother, Park Jihyun

Clan:
Milyang Park, descendants of Prince Pak Ŏnch'im, son of the ruler of the Korean kingdom of Silla in the 10th century

Languages:
Korean, Japanese, some English

Height:
174cm (5ft 8in)

Position in BTS:
vocalist, dancer

Performing at the MBC Gayo Music Festival in Seoul on December 31, 2016.

Ajeong JM, CC BY 4.0 via Wikimedia Commons

> " I want you to smile for real - not one of those smiles that you put on your face to move on with your day, but a real smile from pure happiness in your heart."
> Jimin

Vocal range:
tenor with the ability to hit high notes

Instruments:
guitar

Currently living:
a luxury apartment in the Nine One Hannam complex, decorated in cool blues and browns

Jimin advertising L'Atelier perfume in 2019.

> " Jimin was just so amazing at expressing emotion through dance that I remember thinking, 'Wow, he's good', and then when I heard his voice he had such a beautiful tone I was impressed even more."
> Pdogg, Big Hit Entertainment producer

Social media:
www.instagram.com/j.m/
www.instagram.com/jimin_bighitentertainment/

Inside & Outside Jimin

Military service: December 2023 to June 2025, appointed to serve in an artillery unit

Education:
Graduated in 2014 from the Korea Arts School in Seoul
Degree in Broadcasting & Entertainment from the Global Cyber University in 2020
Enrolled in Master of Business Administration in Advertising & Media course at Hanyang Cyber University in 2021

Endorsement and brand ambassador: Dior fashion and beauty house (2023-date), Tiffany & Co jewelry (2023-date)

Hobbies: reading, gymnastics, taekwondo, collecting art, playing video games

Fav colour: blue

BT21 character: pure-hearted Chimmy, a yellow puppy in a hoodie who always has his tongue poking out and works hard at anything that catches his attention.

Emerging into the afternoon sunlight at the end of his 18-month tour of duty in military service.

BTS 7 tattoo: his left forefinger

Health: has suffered from neck and shoulder cramps, had appendix removed in 2022

Favourite foods: sour things like limes and lemons, Kimchi Jjigae meat and cabbage stew, Samyang Buldak Ramen spicy noodles

Favourite things: Korean romcoms, spending time with friends, travelling

Dislikes: making mistakes onstage, seafood

Bad habits: falling out of chairs, taking a long time to get ready for a performance

Ideal girl: petite, kind, cute

Childhood dreams: to be a policeman or a singer

Personal style: perfectionist, expressive in dance, stylish dresser

Performing at the Mnet Music Awards in Hong Kong in 2014.

What!
Got his nickname Mo-chi - a Japanese rice cake - as he's sweet and squishy

Jimin the High Achiever

Academically and creatively, Jimin has always excelled. He was on the Student Council throughout his school life and Class President for nine years. He was named top student at the Joy Dance Academy and in 2014 he graduated as top student from the Korea Arts School. In 2020 he was presented with the highest honour given by the Global Cyber University, the President's Award, for being an outstanding student.

Thanks to his hard work and attention to detail, his popularity has grown massively with BTS and as a solo star. In 2023 he entered the *Guinness Book of World Records* as the fastest solo K-pop star to gain one billion streams on Spotify.

Jimin's military service was also a big success. First, he was given a commendation as Best Trainee during his initial five weeks and then, during his time in the 5th Infantry Division, he gained an early promotion in rank and was chosen as a Special Class Warrior after only six months' service.

Work outside music

- Has appeared in a number of variety and talk shows such as *After School Club*, *Please Take Care of My Refrigerator*, and *Are You Sure?*

- He has joined in the two BTS addresses to the United Nations Assembly

- 2023 documentary series *Jimin's Production Diary*

Performing on the Grammy Awards broadcast in March 2021.

Theo Wargo/Getty Images

Jimin's Music

Influences: Korean singer Rain, US singers Tori Kelly and Chris Brown

Pre-training: Busan High School of Arts studying in the Department of Dance

Auditions: His Busan dance teacher encouraged him to apply to Big Hit Entertainment and he passed the audition in his home town before they flew him to Seoul to become a trainee

First solo song: *Lie* on the *Wings* album in 2016

First solo release: *Promise* in 2018

Second solo release: *Christmas Love* in 2020

Debut album: *FACE*, a mini-album with seven tracks, in 2023

Second mini-album (seven tracks): *MUSE* in 2024

What! Jimin was only a trainee for six months before he was judged ready to join BTS

"It would be really great if our music continues to touch people. Once your heart is moved, it will develop to something better and positive."

Jimin and RM at the release of the *Be* album in 2020.

The Chosunilbo JNS/Getty Images

Good Causes

2016-2018	covered the uniform costs of students at Busan Hodong Elementary School until it closed in 2018
2019	$72,000 to the Busan Department of Education to support students from low-income families
2020	$72,000 to the Jeonnam Future Education Foundation for a scholarship fund
2021	$72,000 to Rotary International for polio patients
2022	donation to the Gangwon Provincial Office of Education
2023	$72,000 to Korean UNICEF for children affected by the earthquake in southern Turkey and northern Syria
2023	$72,000 to the North Chungcheong Provincial Office of Education to buy books and fund a reading programme
2023	participated in a Hometown Love Donation System to support welfare in Nam District of Busan and donated the allowed maximum of $36,000
2024	$72,000 to the South Gyeongsang Provincial Office of Education to create the scholarships
2024	$72,000 to fund scholarships, living and medical expenses for Korean soldiers
2024	$22,000 to the Busan Habitat Challenge to improve living conditions for the elderly

KIM TAE-HYUNG

김태형

On his way to the airport in June 2022 to take part in Paris Fashion Week as a guest of the Celine Homme Summer show.

The Chosunilbo JNS/Getty Images

Real name:
Kim Tae-hyung

Nicknames:
V, Vante

ARMY call him:
Tae, TaeTae, CGV (computer-generated V, because he is so perfect)

Born:
December 30, 1995 in Daegu, southeast Korea

Grew up:
in Geochang, in south central Korea

Family:
Dad, Daehyun, and mum, Baekhyun; one younger sister, Kim Eun Jin, and one younger brother, Kim Jeon Gyu. Grew up with his grandparents, who were farmers.

Clan:
Gwangsan Kim, descendants of the third son of King Sinmu in the 9th century Korean kingdom of Silla. The same clan as Jin's family.

Languages:
Korean, Japanese, basic sign language, some English

"As V, he uses the freedom he feels with his stage persona to treat every song as a script to which he brings a character to life that expresses his feelings inspired by the song."
Kim Taehyung Global fan-created website

Height:
178cm (5ft 10in)

Position in BTS:
vocalist, composer, visuals

Vocal range:
baritone with husky elements but also able to sing falsetto

Instruments:
saxophone, violin, piano

Currently living:
in a penthouse in SK Apelbaum Flat complex in the Gangnam district of Seoul, with views of the Han River

THE FACT/Getty Images

"I have a big heart full of love so please take it all."
V

Social media:
www.instagram.com/thv/

Inside & Outside V

Attending the Grammy Awards ceremony in Las Vegas in 2022.

What!
He holds a Guinness World Record for the fastest person to gain 10 million followers

Military service: December 2023 to June 2025, assigned to the Special Task Force of the Military Police Corps

Education:
Graduated from Korea Art School in Seoul in 2014
Gained a degree in Broadcasting & Entertainment from the Global Cyber University in 2020
Enrolled at the Hanyang Cyber University in 2021 to study for a Master of Business Administration in Advertising & Media

Endorsement and brand ambassador:
Samsung Galaxy S20 (2022), Cartier Jewelry (2023-date), Celine luxury ready-to-wear (2023-date), SimInvest Indonesian finance company (2023), Compose Coffee (2024), Coca-Cola Korea (2025)

BT21 character: Tata, an alien from Planet BT with a red heart-shaped head and blue body who has superpowers and a hyper-stretchy body.

Hobbies: painting and designing, photography, basketball, cycling, visiting art galleries

Pets: A Pomeranian puppy, Yeontan (aka Tannie), who he adopted in 2017. Tannie was born with breathing and heart problems and died in 2024.

Fav colours: black and white… and purple, of course!

BTS 7 tattoo: on his left leg above the knee

Health: a calf injury prevented him from dancing in the Permission to Dance on Stage concerts

Favourite foods: hot chocolate, Japchae noodles

Favourite things: anime, classical and jazz music, collecting clothes, hats, shoes and jewellery

Dislikes: coffee (despite being a model for a coffee brand), vegetables

Bad habits: biting his nails, touching everything he sees that he thinks is cute

Ideal girl: charming, caring, likes aegyo, likes his parents

Childhood dreams: to be just like his dad

Personal style: artistic, suave, loving, thoughtful

V on the day of his discharge from military service in June 2025.

The Chosunibo JNS

Icon Sportswire/Getty Images

V the Artist

V's alter ego for his creative, non-musical work is Vante, named after the artist Van Gogh and the photographer Ante Badzim. Under that name he has produced expressionist paintings, landscape photographs and custom designs for clothing and jewellery.

"When it came to embodying the magnetism and aura of the panther, our choice naturally fell on V. He has the look and strength of character. A personality whose choices are guided by creativity… with this style and this elegance that belong only to him."

Arnaud Carrez, Senior Vice-President of Cartier jewellery

Work outside music

V was invited to throw the first pitch to start a baseball match between the Cincinnati Reds and the Los Angeles Dodgers in August 2025.

- Acting in historical K-drama *Hwarang: The Poet Warrior Youth*

- Photographed the cover art for his solo release *Winter Bear* in 2019

- He has joined in two addresses at United Nations events

- In 2022 he starred in reality series *In the Soop: Friendcation*

- Appeared in the cooking and travelling show *Jinny's Kitchen* in 2023

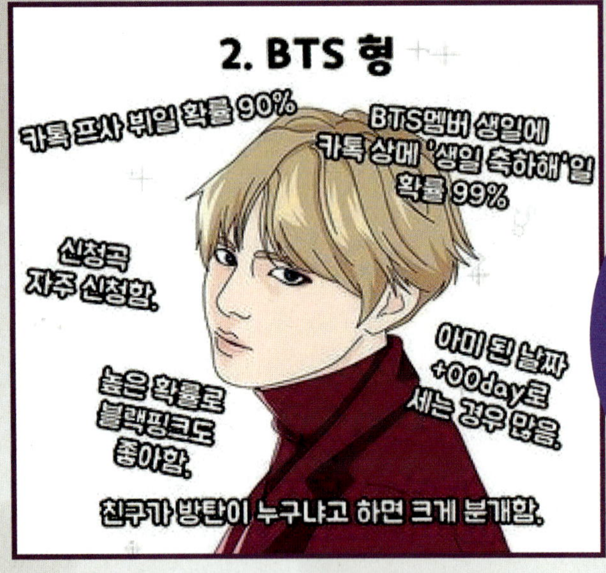

V as depicted in a school textbook giving careers advice.

Saudi Arabia, CC BY 3.0 via Wikimedia Commons

V's Music

Influences: in music, US musicians Ruben Studdard and Eric Benet; in art Vincent Van Gogh, Jean-Michel Basquiat, Egon Schiele

Auditions: Accompanied a friend to Big Hit Entertainment auditions in Daegu and was persuaded to try out himself. After asking his father's permission he became the only person that day to be offered a trainee position.

First solo song: *Stigma* for the *Wings* album in 2016

First solo release: *Scenery* in 2019

Second solo and first English release: *Winter Bear* in 2019 – he used a translation app to write the lyrics

First solo album: *Layover* in 2023

"When things get hard, stop for a while and look back and see how far you've come."
V

What!
His ideal date would be going to an amusement park and holding hands with his partner

Good Causes

2025 | $145,000 to the Korean Red Cross to help relief efforts in the wildfires that devastated three regions of Korea. Other donations, such as during Save The Children, are not made public.

" This dude has some major pipes, and has no problem producing super soothing, low tones that are a key element in the overall sound for BTS."
Journalist Karen Ruffini reporting in *Elite Daily*

JEON JEONG-GUK
전정국

All About Jung Kook

Real name:
Jeon Jeong-guk

Nicknames:
Jung Kook, Golden Maknae (because he is the youngest)

ARMY call him:
JK, Kookie

Born:
September 1, 1997 in Busan, southeast Korea

Family:
Dad, mum and one older brother, Jeon Jung Hyun

Languages:
Korean, English, Japanese

Height:
178cm (5ft 10in)

Position in BTS:
vocalist, visuals

Vocal range:
tenor

Instruments:
guitar, piano, drums

Currently living:
in the Brunnen Cheongdam Villa in the Cheongdam/ Itaewon area of Seoul

"When I was younger, I thought that everything would just come to me eventually, but now I see I have to take the initiative and practise to improve myself."

Michael Loccisano/Getty Images

Appearing on *The Today Show* in the US in 2023.

"Even if I seem to just do things without much forethought or come across as really simplistic, I usually have serious thoughts going on in my head."

Social media:
www.instagram.com/Jung Kook_bighitentertainment/
www.instagram.com/Jung Kook97.back/

www.tiktok.com/@Jung Kook

Inside & Outside Jung Kook

Jung Kook speaking at the United Nations General Assembly in 2021.

Pool/Getty Images News

Divine Treasure, CC BY 4.0 via Wikimedia Commons

Performing at KCON music festival in Los Angeles in 2016.

Military service: December 2023 to June 2025, appointed as a cook in an artillery unit.

Education:
In 2012 he spent the summer training at the Movement Lifestyle dance school in Burbank, California.
Graduated from the School of Performing Arts Seoul in 2017
Gained a degree in Broadcasting & Entertainment from the Global Cyber University in 2022

Endorsements and brand ambassador: Calvin Klein (2023-date)

BT21 character: dependable Cooky, a pink bunny rabbit who's full of energy and heart and will do anything for a friend.

Hobbies: drawing and painting, bowling, football, playing Overwatch video games, cooking

Pets: a red and tan Dobermann dog called Bam who has his own instagram account www.instagram.com/bowwow_bam

Fav colours: red and black

BTS 7 tattoo: behind his left ear

Health: he suffers from rhinitis, which makes him sniff a lot; during the *Love Yourself* tour he injured his foot and had to have stitches in his heel

Favourite foods: pizza, Dwaeji-gukbap (soup from Busan made with pork and rice), bread, sashimi, banana milk

Favourite things: matching his clothes, playing pranks on his fellow band members, doing impressions of them

Dislikes: cigarettes, vegetables, insects (apart from stag beetles), studying, losing at games

Bad habits: bullying his friends, sniffing, not keeping his room tidy

Ideal girl: petite, a good cook, smart, pretty legs, good at singing

Childhood dreams: to be a professional badminton player

Personal style: shy but flirty, careful, perfectionist, very critical of himself

What!
Received Global Cyber University's Presidents' Award, its highest honour, in 2022

Jung Kook the Shy Guy

Although he's known as a bit of a joker and can hassle the other members of BTS, there's a quiet, shy side to Jung Kook and he respects his bandmates very much – even envies their talents and qualities. He has said he admires RM's and Suga's wide ranging knowledge, V's natural talent, J-Hope's positivity, Jimin's dogged persistence and Jin's ability to handle anything that comes his way.

When he first moved into the trainee dorm with the others, he used to take his shower late at night when everyone was asleep so he wouldn't disturb them. He wrote his first song, *Begin*, about how his older BTS friends, his hyungs, had helped him to grow up and he has talked about how they looked after him when he was only 15.

JK is sensitive to criticism and doesn't rate himself very highly. In answer to a question at the 2019 BTS Festa he said he shines brightly on stage with the band but in his everyday life he feels he is insignificant. Not something ARMYs would agree with!

> **"I can't just say 'cheer up no matter what', but in the midst of that difficulty, try to find that small happiness."**

> **"Finding his vocal skills lacking when BTS debuted, Jung Kook began to practise singing at every opportune moment - in the green room, the company car, his hotel room, walking down the street."**
> Monica Kim, *Vogue*

Work outside music

- Appeared in game shows *Celebrity Bromance* and *King of Mask Singer* in 2016

- He has joined in the two addresses at United Nations Assemby with the rest of BTS

- Star of *Jung Kook: I Am Still* documentary movie in 2024

Jung Kook's Music

Influences: US singers Usher, Justin Beiber, Charlie Puth and Justin Timberlake, rapper G-Dragon, Korean singers Zion T and IU

Pre-training: Auditioned for *Superstar K* when the talent show scouts came to Busan in 2011, but he wasn't chosen

Auditions: Didn't audition in the traditional way. He was seen at the talent show auditions and was offered a trainee position by Big Hit Entertainment

First solo song: *Begin* from the album *Wings* in 2016

Second solo song: *Euphoria*, intro to the third of the *Love Yourself* series in 2018

First solo release: *Seven* in July 2023

Second solo release: *3D* in September 2023

First all-English solo album: *Golden* in 2023, which sold more than 2.4 million copies in a week

First solo collaboration: as part of the 'One Dream, One Korea' campaign with other Korean artists in 2015 in memory of the Korean War

What!

His first solo single, *Seven*, was the fastest track in history to reach one billion streams on Spotify

What!

First Korean solo artist to gain three top 10 places in the UK Singles Chart

"I am still curious about people of my age. How they're living, what they're thinking, what are their goals and dreams? What I can do at the moment and be of help to them is music. A song that can encourage and comfort them during hard times."

Duckleavepics, CC BY 4.0 via Wikimedia Commons

Good Causes

2023 | $727,000 to Seoul National University Children's Hospital to cover the cost of treatment for low-income families

2025 | $727,000 to the Hope Bridge Korea Disaster Relief Association for emergency supplies for people affected by wildfires and to improve working conditions for firefighters

ARMYs from all over the world gathered in Goyang, South Korea, for the annual BTS Festa in June 2025.

BTS ARMY:
A Global Community

The BTS ARMY is more than just a big group of fans, it's a close-knit family spread out across the world.

ARMY, of course, stands for Adorable Representative M C for Youth but you can be any age to join – you just have to stand united with other ARMYs in devotion to the Bulletproof Boy Scouts. The name was chosen by BTS to reflect the group's mission to connect with young people everywhere and encourage them to pursue their dreams and stand against prejudice and adversity. In return, ARMY has played a big part in turning the boys from a South Korean sensation to international superstars.

Like soldiers in an actual army, BTS ARMYs have strength, loyalty and solidarity. They're a protective shield, defending the Bangtan Boys and each other against anyone who would harm them.

ARMY Bomb Light Stick

A globe that represents BTS taking over the world is the must-have for concertgoers.

> ## "We are from different countries, we live in different circumstances, but you know we share the same heart and speak the same language."
> RM

Han Myung-Gu/Getty Images

WHY IS ARMY SO SPECIAL?

ARMY arrived on July 9, 2013 and quickly spread. Unlike many pop fandoms limited by geography, language, or cultural boundaries, this is a global community. There are battalions in lots of countries, but they are united under the ARMY name.

The language barrier has been overcome by an infrastructure of fan-run translation services and subtitling teams that make BTS's content available in dozens of languages. You can be in South Korea, Brazil, the UK, India, Spain, the US, or any one of more than 100 countries and you will still be able to take part and share the passion.

WHERE DO YOU FIND ARMY?

ARMY's fandom has a big presence on X, Instagram, TikTok, Weverse and YouTube, sharing stories, photos and opinions, asking questions, giving advice and archiving everything BTS! It's a caring, supportive safe space where everyone has the same goal, to be part of the big Bangtan family.

ARMYs take part in streamed events, fundraising campaigns and voting drives. When BTS music is released there's likely to be a 'streaming party' to boost downloads and run up record-breaking numbers! The same goes for international award shows, such as the American Music Awards or the MTV Europe Music Awards. If there's a public vote ARMY makes sure BTS gets noticed!

"Us and our fans are a great influence on each other. We learn through the process of making music and receiving feedback."
J-Hope

> The ARMY BT21 character is Van, a grey and white space robot with a pointy head who knows everything in the galaxy and is the 24/7 guardian of the BT21 characters

BTS FESTAS AND FAN GET-TOGETHERS

Fan meets are the best places for ARMY to be. Live or online events where ARMYs can interact with each other and their favourite BTS member.

Before Covid-19 and military service there were special Fanmeeting tours and ARMY Musters most years, but these have been on hold since 2022. Maybe 2026 will bring more opportunities for those great in-person concerts? Fingers crossed!

There have, however, been the fabulous two-week BTS Festas every year since 2014, leading up to the anniversary of the group's debut on June 13. Timetables vary but usually feature live radio appearances and internet broadcasts, fresh songs, new portraits and special choreography videos to view. Sometimes fans can attend an online dinner party or see behind the scenes at a photoshoot.

The Festa generally ends with a live concert featuring songs that are not normally performed, special dance numbers, cover versions and a whole lot of BTS joy.

MAKING A POSITIVE IMPACT

It's not just BTS that benefits from the power of ARMY. Far more than just a fan club, it's renowned for doing good, inspired by the boys' messages of kindness, self-acceptance and contributing to society.

ARMY has orchestrated countless charity projects around the world, from fundraising for relief in natural disasters to supporting education, planting trees and donating to mental health organisations.

To mark BTS's anniversaries and birthdays, ARMY often organises global charity drives, raising huge amounts of money for favourite causes. In June 2020, in less than 24 hours, ARMY had matched BTS's $1 million

> ❝ **The heart that thinks of ARMY and the pencil that wrote my story belongs to you, and I will never forget that.** ❞
> Jung Kook, writing to fans while on military service

Fans attending the 2025 BTS Festa in Goyang, celebrating the boys completing their military service.

donation to the Black Lives Matter movement. That huge achievement showed not only ARMYs' efficiency but their commitment to supporting social justice.

In 2023, to celebrate 10 years of BTS adoration, some fans came together to write a song for BTS called *Love Letters*, which can be seen on YouTube. All proceeds from the downloads were donated to charity.

It's not just about raising money, though. ARMY volunteers also give a lot of time to community projects and environmental campaigns. It's all about contributing to BTS's mission.

BTS On Tour:
The Red Bullet

Only a year after their official debut, BTS was on tour, showing the world what the boys were all about.

When:

October 2014 to August 2015

Showcasing:

2 Cool 4 Skool album

O!RUL8,2? EP

Skool Luv Affair EP

Dark & Wild album

Number of concerts:

22

Locations:

- Seoul, South Korea
- Kobe and Tokyo, Japan
- Pasay City, Philippines
- Singapore
- Bangkok and Pak Kret, Thailand
- Taipei, Taiwan
- Kuala Lumpur, Malaysia
- Sydney and Melbourne, Australia
- New York, Grand Prairie Texas, Rosemont Illinois, Los Angeles California, USA
- Mexico City
- São Paulo, Brazil
- Santiago, Chile
- Hong Kong

Total attendance:

80,000

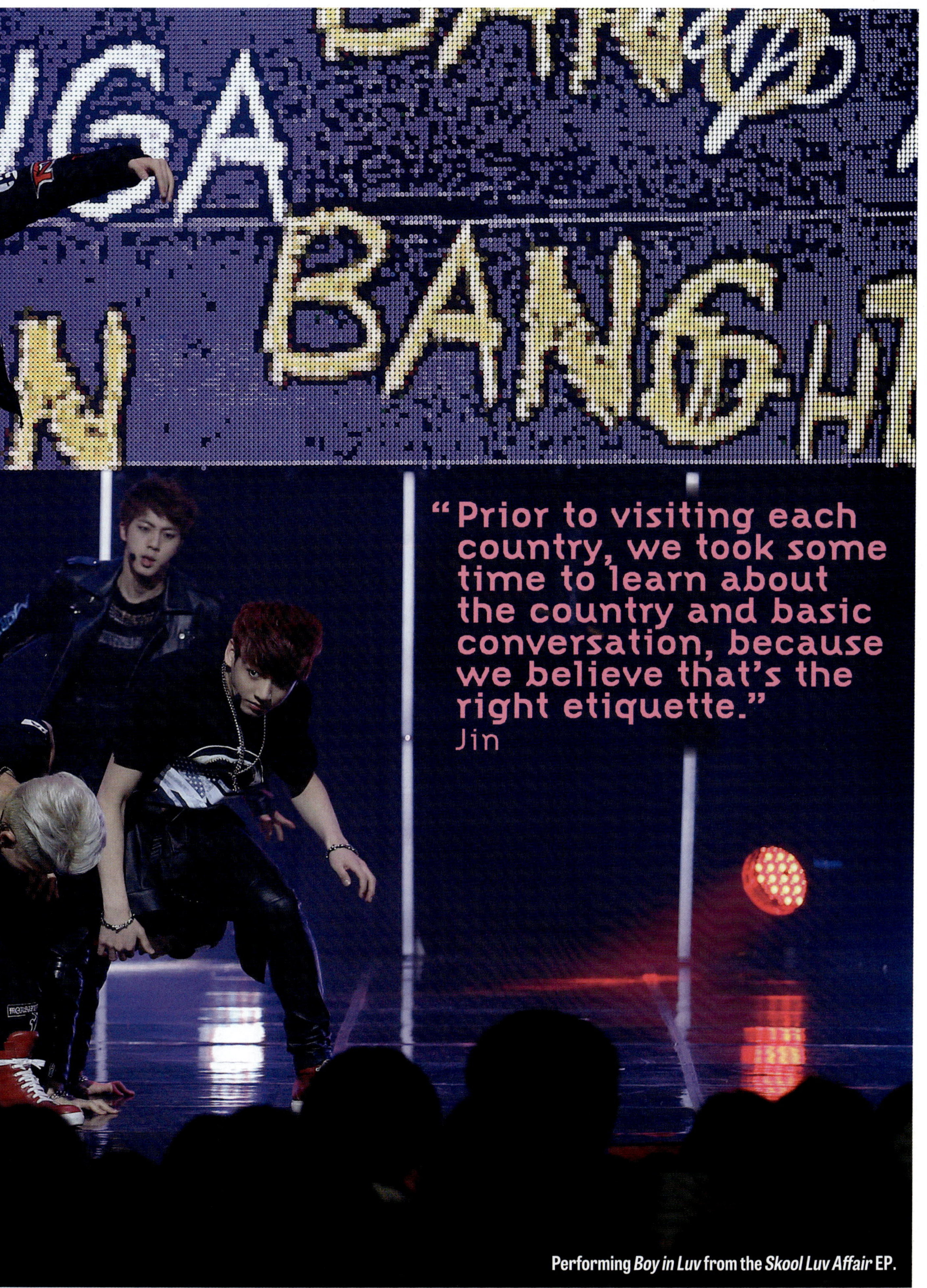

"Prior to visiting each country, we took some time to learn about the country and basic conversation, because we believe that's the right etiquette."
Jin

Performing *Boy in Luv* from the *Skool Luv Affair* EP.

Onstage at the SBS Prism Tower in Seoul in 2015.

"We're not sure if we've actually earned respect. But one thing for sure is that [people] feel this is not just some kind of a syndrome, a phenomenon. These little boys from Korea are doing this."
RM

BTS On Tour: Wake Up – Open Your Eyes

The group's huge popularity in Japan was recognised with the release of their Japanese album *Wake Up* and an accompanying tour.

When:

February 2015

Showcasing:

Wake Up album

Locations:

- Chiba
- Osaka
- Nagoya
- Fukuoka

Number of concerts:

6

Total attendance:

25,000

BTS On Tour: The Most Beautiful Moment In Life

The Most Beautiful Moment trilogy took the group all around Asia and their biggest audience yet.

When:

November 2015 to August 2016

Showcasing:

The Most Beautiful Moment in Life Pt 1 album

The Most Beautiful Moment in Life Pt 2 album

The Most Beautiful Moment in Life – Young Forever album

Number of concerts:

22

Locations:

Seoul, South Korea

Yokohama, Kobe, Osaka, Nagoya and Tokyo, Japan

New Taipei City, Taiwan

Macau, Nanjing and Beijing, China

Pasay City, Philippines

Bangkok, Thailand

Total attendance:

182,500

"Watching so many fans in different countries recognizing our songs and singing them along in Korean lyrics was a very special experience."
Suga

Showcasing *The Most Beautiful Moment In Life* trilogy in 2016.

BTS On Tour: The Wings Tour

This gave BTS a huge jump in audience numbers, reaching over 100,000 people more than their first tour – a measure of how the world was embracing the magnificent seven.

When:

February 2017 to December 2017

Showcasing:

Wings album

You Never Walk Alone repackaged album

Number of concerts:

40

Locations:

 Seoul, South Korea

 Santiago, Chile

 São Paulo, Brazil

 Newark New Jersey, Rosemont Illinois and Anaheim California, USA

 Bangkok, Thailand

Tangerang, Indonesia

 Pasay City, Philippines

 Hong Kong

Sydney, Australia

 Osaka, Hiroshima, Nagoya, Saitama, Fukuoka and Sapporo, Japan

 Taoyuan, Taiwan

Macau, China

Total attendance:

550,000

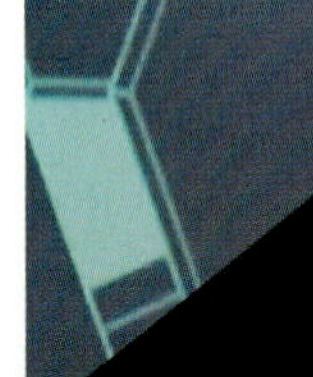

Jung Kook salutes the crowd in the stadium at Newark, New Jersey in March 2017.

Divine Treasure, CC BY 4.0 via Wikimedia Commons

"The concert that we had in Brazil was particularly impressive… it was mesmerizing to see the entire venue completely filled up with our fans."
Jung Kook

BTS On Tour: Love Yourself

This tour gave Europeans their first chance to see the full spectacle of BTS, paving the way, we hope, for even more concerts in Europe in 2026.

When:

August 2018 to October 2019

Showcasing:

Love Yourself – Her, Tear album

Answer compilation album

Map of the Soul – Persona EP

Number of concerts:

62

Locations:

 Seoul, South Korea

 Los Angeles and Oakland California, Fort Worth Texas, Newark New Jersey, Chicago Illinois and New York, USA

 Hamilton, Canada

 London, UK

 Amsterdam, Netherlands

Berlin, Germany

Paris, France

 Tokyo, Osaka, Nagoya and Fukuoka, Japan

 Taoyuan, Taiwan

 Singapore

 Hong Kong

Bangkok, Thailand

Total attendance:
2,019,800

Before moving on to Europe and Asia, BTS hit New York City in 2019.

John Lamparski/Getty Images

"BTS have become artists performing
in those huge stadiums and selling
millions of albums... but I am still
an ordinary 24-year-old guy."
RM

BTS On Tour: Permission To Dance

The Covid-19 pandemic changed the way that BTS was able to perform for their fans.

BTS had originally planned a *Map Of The Soul* tour that would have seen them perform 39 shows, but this had to be cancelled. By the end of 2021, some countries had opened up to theatrical performances again so the group mixed concerts played to small in-person audiences with events held in empty venues. The latter were streamed live online as pay-per-view or screened in theatres worldwide where live audiences were allowed.

The live concerts were not only limited in numbers: ARMYs who were fortunate to go were instructed that they must not cheer their idols, scream or sing along. How hard that must have been!

When:
October 2021 to April 2022

Showcasing:
Be album
Proof anthology album
A number of newly written tracks

Locations:
Seoul, South Korea
Inglewood and Paradise California, and Las Vegas Nevada, USA

Number of concerts:
16

Total attendance:
4 million
made up of in-person and online audiences

The Covid-19 pandemic limited BTS to online concerts and a handful of live performances of their hits such as *Dynamite*.

BBMA2020/Getty Images

"Going back on tour, going back on track and seeing all the fans and people finally in two years, it really made us feel like this really is the beginning of our new chapter... the past two years of the pandemic weren't easy..."
RM

Record Breakers!

The Bangtan Boys have racked up some pretty big numbers in their careers so far. Here's a few to blow your minds.

No 1
Billboard Top 100 artist chart in 2018 (1st Koreans to reach that psition)

45.9 million
Views of *Idol* video in first 24 hours on YouTube

7
Awards in the 2018 Korean Melon Music Awards

9
Wins in the 2018 Mnet Asian Music Awards

74.6 million
YouTube views of *Map of the Soul: Persona* video in first 24 hours in 2019

1 million
Instant followers when BTS joined TikTok in 2019

756,600

Fans tuning into the 2020 *Bang Bang Con: The Live* virtual concert

101.1 million

YouTube views of *Dynamite* in 24 hours in August 2020

13+ billion

Number of video views to date through Big Hit Labels on YouTube

191

Countries where BTS fans streamed *Map of the Soul: ON:E* concert in October 2020

1st

Korean band ever to have a song and album *(Be)* in *Billboard* charts in the same week

1.4 billion

Streams of *Butter* on Spotify since May 2021

13

Guinness World Records for music and social media broken in 2021 alone

214,000

Tickets sold for Los Angeles *Permission to Dance* On Stage concerts in 2021

15 million

Web views of BTS comic *7Fates: Chakho* in two days in 2022

3

Guinness World Records in March 2022 for most-followed group on TikTok, Twitter and Instagram

40 million

Albums sold to date – making BTS the best-selling music act in Korean history

$4.65 billion

Annual value of BTS to the South Korean economy

BTS: The Albums

BTS's style has branched out from hip-hop to cover a wide range of musical genres, and their albums have been smash hits around the world.

Ilgan Sports/Getty Images

I n all their songs BTS really speaks to ARMY, with lyrics about the kinds of things everyone faces – good and bad relationships, education, finding your place in the world, fear of the future and, especially, how you have to love yourself and make the most of your life.

The group members co-write and produce most of the tracks on their albums, along with the Big Hit producers. They create themes that are often told over three-part stories.

You can stream all the albums over a variety of services:
open.spotify.com/
music.youtube.com/
music.amazon.com/
tidal.com/
vibe.naver.com/
music.bugs.co.kr/
www.deezer.com/
www.genie.co.kr/
www.music-flo.com
www.melon.com/
Apple Music

Or you can buy the physical albums, which come with the same track lists but with different versions of cover art and photocard extras. Plus, you get additional songs (called hidden tracks) that don't feature on the streamed versions.

2 Cool 4 Skool
BTS's first album in their *Skool* trilogy.

Release Date: 12 June 2013

Promoted single: *We Are Bulletproof Pt 2*

Track List:

Intro: 2 Cool 4 Skool (featuring DJ Friz)

We Are Bulletproof Pt 2

Skit: Circle Room Talk

No More Dream

Interlude

Like

Outro: Circle Room Cypher

Hidden Track: Skit: On The Start Line

Hidden Track: Path

O!RUL8,2?
BTS's first mini album and the second work in their *Skool* trilogy

Release Date: 11 September 2013
Promoted single: *Attack on Bangtan*

Track List:

Intro: O!RUL8,2?

N.O

Attack on Bangtan

Coffee

We On

Skit: R U Happy Now?

If I Ruled The World

Paldogangsan/Satoori Rap

BTS Cypher Pt 1

Outro: Luv In Skool

Skool Luv Affair
Second mini album and the third set of songs in the *Skool* trilogy

Release Date: 13 February 2014
Promoted single: *Just One Day*

Track List:

Intro: Skool Luv Affair

Boy In Luv

Skit: Soulmate

Where You From?

Just One Day

Tomorrow

BTS Cypher Pt 2: Triptych

Spine Breaker

Jump

Outro: Propose

Onstage with the *Skool* Trilogy in 2014.

" ... a culmination of the '*Skool* Trilogy' project that discusses the topics of most interest to teens their own age - dreams, happiness and love. Such penetrating insight into the hearts and minds of young people led to the absolute support that BTS has received from fans their age."
Big Hit Music

Skool Luv Affair Special Addition

A limited edition based on the last album in the *Skool* Trilogy which includes new tracks and a number of hidden tracks in the physical album.

Release Date: 15 May 2014
Promoted Single: *Just One Day*

Track List:

Miss Right

Like (Slow Jam Remix)

Intro: Skool Luv Affair

Boy In Luv

Skit: Soulmate

Where You From?

Just One Day

Tomorrow

BTS Cypher Pt 2: Triptych

Spine Breaker

Jump (Follow-up Track)

Outro: Propose

Hidden Track: Boy In Luv Instrumental

Hidden Track: Where You From? Instrumental

Hidden Track: Just One Day Instrumental

Hidden Track: Tomorrow Instrumental

Hidden Track: Spine Breaker Instrumental

Hidden Track: Jump Instrumental

Ilgan Sports/Getty Images

Dark & Wild
BTS's first studio album.

Release Date: 21 August 2014

Promoted Single: *War Of Hormone*

Track List:

Intro: What Am I To You

Danger

War of Hormone

Hip Hop Phile

Let Me Know

Rain

BTS Cypher Pt 3: Killer (featuring Supreme Boi)

Interlude: What Are You Doing Now?

Could You Turn Off Your Cell Phone?

Embarrassed

24/7 = Heaven

Look Here

Second Grade

Outro: Do You Think It Makes Sense?

The Most Beautiful Moment In Life Pt 1
BTS's third mini album and the first instalment in the *Beautiful Moment* trilogy.

Release Date: 30 April 2015

Album Versions:
Pink [CD + Photobook + Random Photocard]
White [CD + Photobook + Random Photocard]

Promoted single: *Dope*

Track List:

Intro: The Most Beautiful Moment in Life

I Need U

Hold Me Tight

Skit: Expectation!

Dope

Boyz With Fun

Converse High

Moving On

Outro: Love is Not Over

Showcasing *Dark & Wild* at Blue Square in Seoul the month the album is released in 2014.

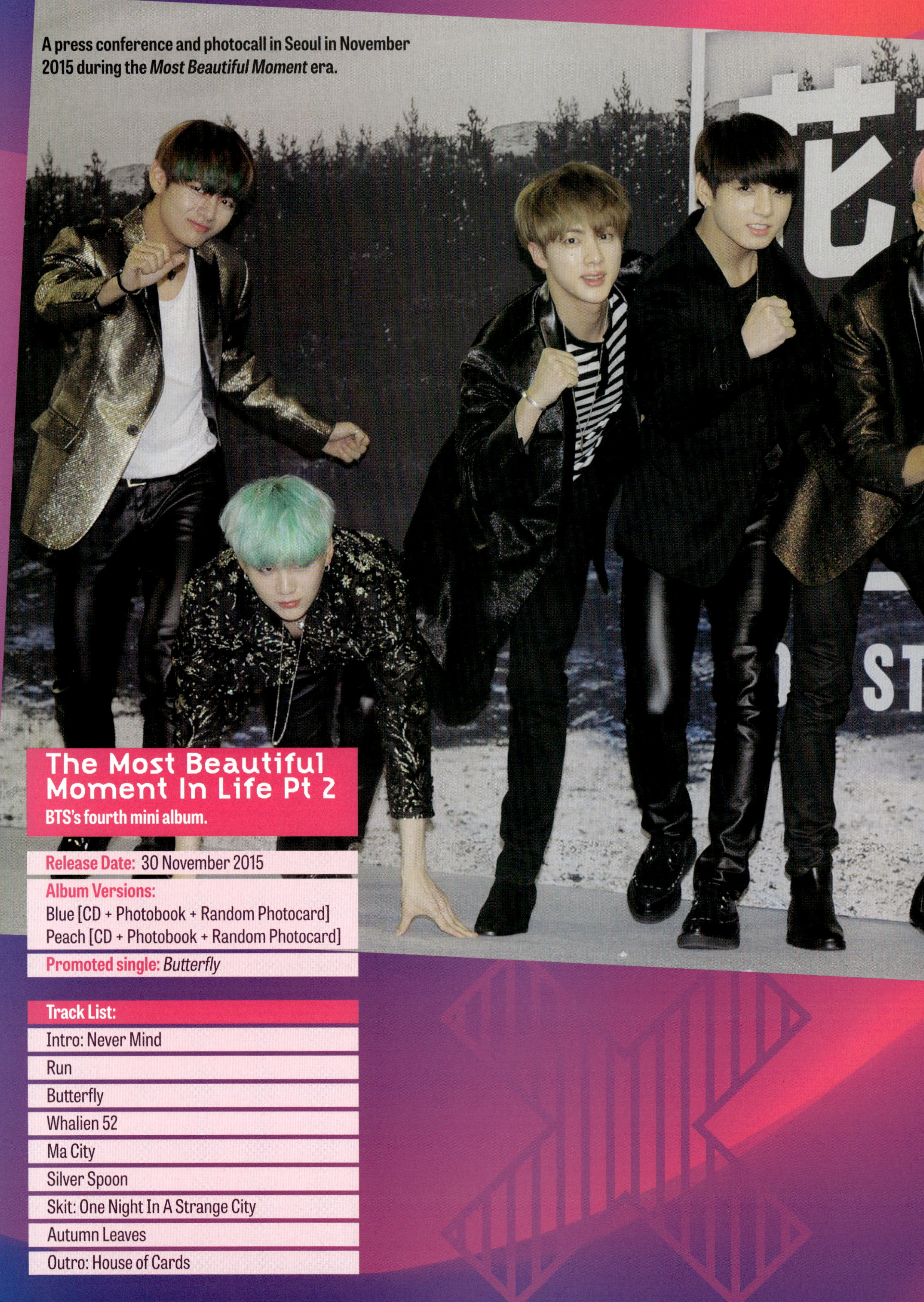

A press conference and photocall in Seoul in November 2015 during the *Most Beautiful Moment* era.

The Most Beautiful Moment In Life Pt 2
BTS's fourth mini album.

Release Date: 30 November 2015

Album Versions:
Blue [CD + Photobook + Random Photocard]
Peach [CD + Photobook + Random Photocard]

Promoted single: *Butterfly*

Track List:

Intro: Never Mind

Run

Butterfly

Whalien 52

Ma City

Silver Spoon

Skit: One Night In A Strange City

Autumn Leaves

Outro: House of Cards

The Chosunilbo JNS/Getty Images

The Most Beautiful Moment In Life: Young Forever

BTS's first Special Album containing tracks from the first two mini albums in the *Beautiful Moment* trilogy, along with new songs and remixes.

Release Date: 2 May 2016

Album Versions:
Day [2 CDs + Photobook + Random Photocard]
Night [2 CDs + Photobook + Random Photocard]

Promoted single: *Fire, Save Me* and *Epilogue: Young Forever*

Track List:

CD 1

Intro: The Most Beautiful Moment in Life

I Need U

Hold Me Tight

Autumn Leaves

Butterfly (Prologue Remix)

Run

Ma City

Silver Spoon

Dope

Fire

Save Me

Epilogue: Young Forever

CD 2

Converse High

Moving On

Whalien 52

Butterfly

House of Cards (full length version)

Love is Not Over (full length version)

I Need U (Urban mix)

I Need U (Remix)

Run (Ballad mix)

Run (Alternative mix)

Butterfly (Alternative mix)

Wings

BTS's second full-length album.

Release Date: 10 October 2016

Album Versions:
W [CD + Photobook + Random Photocard]
I [CD + Photobook + Random Photocard]
N [CD + Photobook + Random Photocard]
G [CD + Photobook + Random Photocard]
Left [CD + Photobook + Random Photocard]
issued in February 2017
Right [CD + Photobook + Random Photocard]
issued in February 2017

Promoted single: *Am I Wrong* and *21st Century Girl*

Track List:

Intro: Boy Meets Evil

Blood Sweat & Tears

Begin (Jung Kook solo)

Lie (Jimin solo)

Stigma (V solo)

First Love (Suga solo)

Reflection (RM solo)

Mama (J-Hope solo)

Awake (Jin solo)

Lost

BTS Cypher 4

Am I Wrong

21st Century Girl

2! 3!

Interlude: Wings

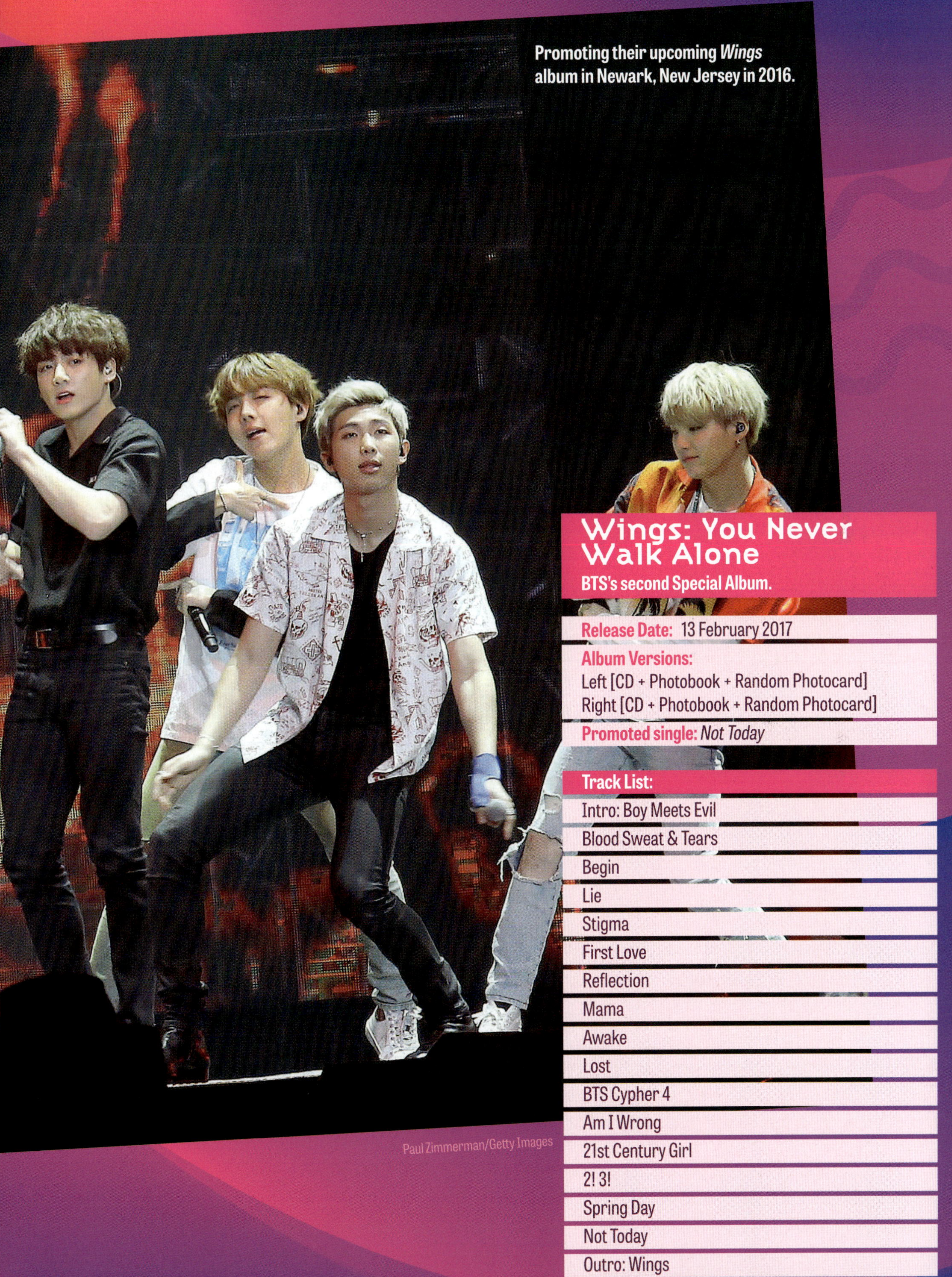

Paul Zimmerman/Getty Images

Wings: You Never Walk Alone
BTS's second Special Album.

Release Date: 13 February 2017

Album Versions:
Left [CD + Photobook + Random Photocard]
Right [CD + Photobook + Random Photocard]

Promoted single: *Not Today*

Track List:

Intro: Boy Meets Evil

Blood Sweat & Tears

Begin

Lie

Stigma

First Love

Reflection

Mama

Awake

Lost

BTS Cypher 4

Am I Wrong

21st Century Girl

2! 3!

Spring Day

Not Today

Outro: Wings

A Supplemental Story: You Never Walk Alone

Love Yourself: Her
BTS's fifth mini album.

Michael Tran/Getty Images

Release Date: 18 September 2017

Album Versions:
L [CD + Photobook + Random Photocard +
The Notes (L) + Sticker Pack]
O [CD + Photobook + Random Photocard +
The Notes (O) + Sticker Pack]
V [CD + Photobook + Random Photocard +
The Notes (V) + Sticker Pack]
E [CD + Photobook + Random Photocard +
The Notes (E) + Sticker Pack]
Vinyl [Outer sleeve + Vinyl + Lyric poster + Poster +
Sticker + Bookmark + Photocard]

Promoted single: *Mic Drop* and *Go (Go Go)*

Track List:

Intro: Serendipity

DNA

Best of Me

Dimple

Pied Piper

Skit: Billboard Music Awards Speech

Mic Drop

Go (Go Go)

Outro: Her

Hidden Track: Skit: Hesitation and Fear
Hidden Track: Sea

Performing *DNA* from the *Love Yourself: Her* album at the American Music Awards event in 2017.

Love Yourself: Tear
BTS's third full-length album

Release Date: 18 May 2018

Album Versions:
Y [CD + Photobook + Random Photocard + The Notes (Y) + Standing Photo]
O [CD + Photobook + Random Photocard + The Notes (O) + Standing Photo]
U [CD + Photobook + Random Photocard + The Notes (U) + Standing Photo]
R [CD + Photobook + Random Photocard + The Notes (R) + Standing Photo]
Vinyl [Outer sleeve + Vinyl + Booklet + Sticker Set + Post Card + Hologram Photocard]

Promoted single: *Airplane Pt 2* and *Anpanman*

Track List:

Intro: Singularity

Fake Love

The Truth Untold (featuring Steve Aoki)

134340

Paradise

Love Maze

Magic Shop

Airplane Pt 2

Anpanman

So What

Outro: Tear

Love Yourself: Answer
BTS repackaged album.

Release Date: 24 August 2018

Album Versions:
S [2 CDs + Photobook + Random Photocard + The Notes (S) + Sticker Pack]
E [2 CDs + Photobook + Random Photocard + The Notes (E) + Sticker Pack]
L [2 CDs + Photobook + Random Photocard + The Notes (L) + Sticker Pack]
F [2 CDs + Photobook + Random Photocard + The Notes (F) + Sticker Pack]

Promoted single: *I'm Fine*

Track List:

CD 1

Euphoria (Jung Kook solo)

Trivia: Just Dance (J-Hope solo)

Serendipity (Jimin solo full length edition)

DNA

Dimple

Trivia: Love (RM solo)

Her

Singularity (V solo)

Fake Love

The Truth Untold (featuring Steve Aoki)

Trivia: Seesaw (Suga solo)

Tear

Epiphany (Jin solo)

I'm Fine

Idol

Answer: Love Myself

CD 2

Magic Shop

Best of Me

Airplane Pt 2

Go (Go Go)

Anpanman

Mic Drop

DNA (Pedal 2 LA Mix)

Fake Love (Rocking Vibe Mix)

Mic Drop (Steve Aoki Remix full length edition)

Digital Only: Idol (featuring Nicki Minaj)

I DARE U JK, CC BY 3.0 via Wikimedia Commons

Map of the Soul: Persona

BTS's sixth mini album.

Release Date: 12 April 2019

Album Versions:
01 [CD + Photobook + Random Photocard + The Notes (1) + Postcard + Photo Film]
02 [CD + Photobook + Random Photocard + The Notes (2) + Postcard + Photo Film]
03 [CD + Photobook + Random Photocard + The Notes (3) + Postcard + Photo Film]
04 [CD + Photobook + Random Photocard + The Notes (4) + Postcard + Photo Film]

Promoted single: *Dionysus*

Track List:

Intro: Persona (RM solo)

Boy With Luv (featuring Halsey)

Mikrokosmos

Make It Right (co-written with Ed Sheeran)

Home

Jamais Vu

Dionysus

Map of the Soul: 7
BTS's fourth full-length studio album

Release Date: 21 February 2020

Album Versions:

01 [CD + Photobook + Lyric Book + Random Photocard + The Notes (1) + Postcard + Sticker + Colouring Paper]
02 [CD + Photobook + Lyric Book + Random Photocard + The Notes (2) + Postcard + Sticker + Colouring Paper]
03 [CD + Photobook + Lyric Book + Random Photocard + The Notes (3) + Postcard + Sticker + Colouring Paper]
04 [CD + Photobook + Lyric Book + Random Photocard + The Notes (4) + Postcard + Sticker + Colouring Paper]

Promoted single: *Black Swan*

Track List:

Intro: Persona
Boy With Luv (featuring Halsey)
Make It Right
Jamais Vu
Dionysus
Interlude: Shadow (Suga solo)
Black Swan
Filter (Jimin solo)
My Time (Jung Kook solo)
Louder Than Bombs
On
Ugh!
00:00 (Zero O'Clock)
Inner Child (V solo)
Friends
Moon (Jin solo)
Respect
We are Bulletproof: The Eternal
Outro: Ego (J-Hope solo)

Digital only: On (featuring Sia)

Rich Fury/Getty Images

> **" Dynamite is an exciting and light-hearted song that we had always wanted to try."**
> RM

Be

BTS's first self-directed mini album with Jimin acting as music project manager and V as visual project manager.

Release Date: 20 November 2020

Album Versions:
Deluxe Edition [CD + Photobook + Making Book + Lyric Poster + 8 Photocards + Polaroid Photocard + Photo Frame + 7 Postcards]
Essential Edition [CD + Photobook + 7 Photocards + Random Photocard + Poster]

Promoted single: *Dynamite*

Track List:
Life Goes On
Fly to my Room
Blue & Grey
Skit
Telepathy
Dis-ease
Stay
Dynamite

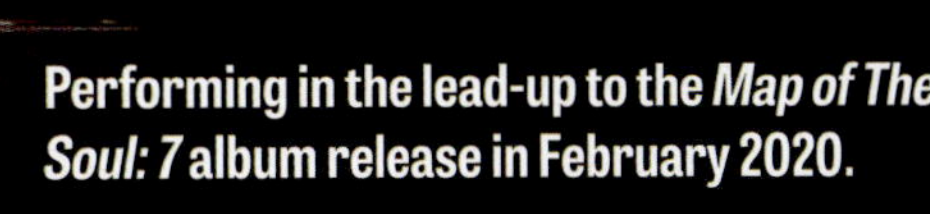

Performing in the lead-up to the *Map of The Soul: 7* album release in February 2020.

Proof
BTS's first anthology album.

Release Date: 10 June 2022

Album Versions:
Standard Edition [3 CDs + The Art of Proof + Photograph + Epilogue + Lyrics + Photocard A (set of 7) + Photocard B (1 random) + Postcard (1 random) + Poster (first press only)]
Compact Edition [3 CDs + Booklet + CD Plate + Photocard (1 random) + Postcard (1 random) + Mini Poster + Discography Guide] | Collector's Edition [3 CDs + Book + Premium Photos (set of 7) + AR Card (set of 7) + 3D Card (set of 7) + Photocard A (set of 7) + Photocard B (set of 7) + User Guide (AR Card, 3D Card)]

Promoted single: *For Youth*

Track List:

CD 1

Born Singer

No More Dream

N.O

Boy In Luv

Danger

I Need U

Run

Fire

Blood Sweat & Tears

Spring Day

DNA

Fake Love

Idol

Boy With Luv (featuring Halsey)

On

Dynamite

Life Goes On

Butter

Yet To Come (The Most Beautiful Moment)

CD 2

Run BTS

Intro: Persona (RM solo)

Stay

Moon (Jin solo)

Jamais Vu

Trivia: Seesaw (Suga solo)

BTS Cypher Pt 3: Killer (featuring Supreme Boi)

Outro: Ego (J-Hope solo)

Her

Filter (Jimin solo)

Friends

Singularity (V solo)

00:00 (Zero O'Clock)

Euphoria (Jung Kook solo)

Dimple

CD 3 (physical CD only)

Jump (demo version)

Young Love

Boy In Luv (demo version)

Quotation Mark

I Need U (demo version)

Boyz with Fun (demo version)

Tony Montana (with Jimin)

Young Forever (RM demo version)

Spring Day (V demo version)

DNA (J-Hope demo version)

Epiphany (Jin demo version)

Seesaw (instrumental demo version)

Still With You (Jung Kook acapella solo)

For Youth

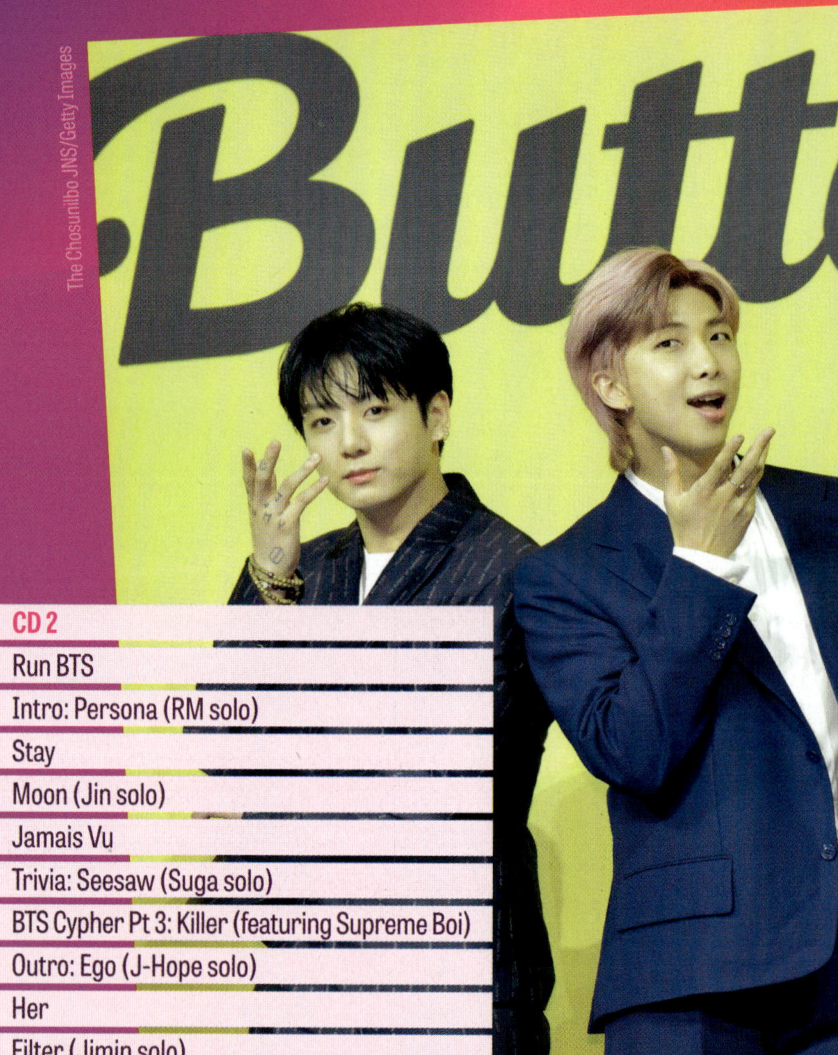

The Chosunilbo JNS/Getty Images

English language hit *Butter* featured as a digital single as well as a track on the *Proof* anthology.

Permission To Dance On Stage – Live

BTS's first live album, recorded as the Covid-19 lockdown was ending when they were able to hold some in-person concerts.

Release Date: 18 July 2025

Album Versions:

Contact [CD + Outer Box + Memo + Photo Note + CD Envelope + Lyric Book + Bookmark + Photocard + Postcards (set if 7)]

Connect [CD + Outer Box + Memo + Photo Note + CD Envelope + Lyric Book + Bookmark + Photocard + Postcard (set of 7)]

Track List:

- On
- Burning Up (Fire)
- Dope
- DNA
- Blue & Grey
- Black Swan
- Blood Sweat & Tears
- Fake Love
- Life Goes On
- Boy With Luv (featuring Halsey)
- Dynamite
- Butter
- Telepathy
- Outro: Wings
- Stay
- So What
- Idol
- Airplane Pt 2
- Silver Spoon
- Dis-ease
- Spring Day
- Permission to Dance

> " **The [Permission To Dance On Stage – Live] album encapsulates the heat of the stage, roaring cheers, and unforgettable memories shared between BTS and ARMY. Featuring 22 live tracks, the album preserves the vivid emotions and excitement that defined each night of the tour.** "
>
> Big Hit Music

Going It Alone

Thanks to the encouragement of Big Hit Entertainment, RM, Jin, Jimin, Suga, V, J-Hope and Jung Kook have been able to explore their own individual music outside of the group.

The break for military service gave the space for all the BTS members to explore their musical styles and lay down some memorable tracks before they came together again to work on their 2026 BTS album.

Some, like RM and Suga had already recorded solo albums – Suga under the name Agust D – but for the others it was a new experience. Not since their pre-trainee days had they worked without their band members around them all the time. That didn't hold them back, though, as they set out to showcase their individuality, and ARMYs will agree they all made a big impression. If you missed any of them, here's the complete rundown of the solo performances of the Bangtan Boys.

RM: Hip-Hop, Poetry and Philosophy

RM, his debut mixtape in 2015, was based on being two sided – depicted by his face being painted half black and half white on the album cover. Everyone is positive sometimes and negative at others, but in the end you are always the same person. RM felt this was summed up in the track *Do You*.

mono in 2018 had a playlist that has been critically acclaimed for its emotional depth and musical diversity, showing RM's thoughtfulness and growth as an artist.

Indigo, RM's first official solo album in 2022, was a reflection of him during his late 20s. It featured collaborations with US singers Erykah Badu, Anderson .Paak, British singer Mahalia and several fellow South Koreans such as Park Ji-yoon and Kin Sa-wol.

Right Place, Wrong Person, RM's second solo studio album, was released in 2024. It came about as a result of a trip to Spain but did not come out until after he had begun his military service term.

Suga as his alter ego Agust D in the music video of *Daechwita*.

Suga: Modern Meets Traditional

Agust D, Suga's first mixtape, released in 2016, was given the name of his alter ego and tackled topics such as handling fame, mental health, and personal struggles in songs such as *The Last*, *So Far Away* and *Give It To Me*.

D-2 in 2020, was a second mixtape that blended traditional Korean sounds with hip-hop and rap. Tracks such as *Daechwita* alternated ancient instruments with strident rap. The project was praised for its originality.

D-Day was Suga's first official studio album, released in 2023 under the name Agust D. It continued his focus on storytelling through music and blending traditional with modern.

J-Hope: Hip-hop, Pop and Rock

Hope World was J-Hope's debut mixtape in 2018 and it was full of creativity and positivity. There were playful songs such as *Daydream* and *Airplane* and artistic ones such as *Blue Side*. The video for *Airplane* gained two million views in under five hours.

Chicken Noodle Soup from 2019 was a fun collaboration with US singer Becky G with an earworm chorus.

Jack In The Box in 2022 was J-Hope's first studio album and surprised listeners with its rock influences and dark themes.

Hope On The Street Vol 1 was a soundtrack album in 2024 for J-Hope's six-part documentary film *Hope On The Street* and featured artists from both South Korea and overseas.

J-Hope performing solo at the Lollapalooza festival in Chicago in 2022.

Gary Miller/Getty Images

Jin lit up the Empire State Building in New York purple to promote his second album *Echo* in May 2025.

Eugene Gologursky/Getty Images

Jin: Calm, Emotive Ballads

Tonight was Jin dipping a toe in the solo world in 2019 with a sentimental ballad about feelings of loss.

Abyss was a single that came out the following year, 2020. It is a soulful ballad reflecting the difficult times of lockdown in Covid-19.

Yours was released in November 2021 to accompany the K-drama series *Jirisan*, about a ranger with psychic powers who sets out to rescue people who are trapped on Mount Jiri.

Super Tuna, released a month after *Yours*, was a much more light-hearted single celebrating fishing and cooking.

The Astronaut in 2022 was his solo single released just before he began his military service. The song was co-written with UK band Coldplay and features an acoustic guitar with a gradual build-up of synth sounds.

Happy in November 2024 was Jin's debut solo album containing six tracks, including *Running Wild*, featuring a collaboration with Gary Barlow of Take That.

Echo, his second album, was released in May 2025 with seven tracks, including *Don't Say You Love Me*.

Jimin: Vulnerability and Artistic Depth

Promise was Jimin's debut single in 2018 that spoke about finding inner strength and therefore happiness.

Christmas Love, released on Christmas Eve in 2020, celebrated youth and innocence.

With You featured in the K-drama series *Our Blues* and was recorded in collaboration with fellow Korean singer Ha Sung-Woon.

FACE, a debut mini album from Jimin in 2023, tackled issues of self-awareness, insecurity and change, with seven tracks that blend pop, R&B and synth sounds.

Closer Than This was released in December 2023 and was Jimin's tribute to ARMY, delivered while he was away from them on military service.

MUSE in 2024 was his second mini album and over the course of its seven tracks it tells the story of looking for genuine love and losing his way, finding inspiration from his surroundings. His solo material is marked by Jimin's willingness to experiment with vocal styles and reveal his fragility as well as his strength.

Jimin showing his artistic side at a fan meet.

Jimson Weed, CC BY 4.0 via Wikimedia Commons

Smooth, romantic vibes inspired by jazz and R&B from V.

V: Nostalgia and Soulful Sounds

Scenery was V's debut solo single in 2019 and is all about longing for someone, something or somewhere else, as you're walking through different surroundings.

Winter Bear, also released in 2019, talked about losing your beloved and the search to find them.

Snow Flower, a solo single released on Christmas Eve 2020, featured V's rapper friend Peakboy.

Christmas Tree went hand-in-hand with the K-drama series *Our Beloved Summer* in 2021, a story of an estranged couple who meet again when the documentary they shot together goes viral.

*Layove*r, V's mini album from 2023, drew inspiration from jazz, R&B and lo-fi pop. Its six tracks, such as *Rainy Days*, *Love Me Again* and *Slow Dancing*, highlighted V's willingness to explore vulnerability and nostalgia and earned him critical acclaim.

Fri(end)s, released in 2024 is a solo song about being stuck between two realities.

Jung Kook: Global Pop Star

Still With You was Jung Kook's first solo single. It was supposed to be released in 2020 at that year's BTS Festa, but Covid-19 prevented that.

My You was the next solo track Jung Kook produced for BTS Festa, this time in 2022, and was written to celebrate the group's relationship with ARMY.

Stay Alive came out in 2022 to be included in BTS' webtoon manga series, *7Fates: Chakho* about seven young men who hunt demon tigers.

Dreamers was performed live at the opening of the FIFA World Cup in Qatar in 2022.

GOLDEN is Jung Kook's debut solo album, released in 2023. It blended pop and R&B with dance music. The album's previously released and successful single, *Seven* (featuring Latto), contrasted with the disco funk track *Standing Next To You*. The album showcased Jung Kook's striking vocals and catchy melodies, and the way he can adapt to different musical genres. The accompanying video confirmed his vibrant stage presence and professional polish.

Jung Kook leads his backing dancers in a New York solo performance in July 2023.

BTS: Solo Tours

With so much material to share, it made sense for three of BTS to take their individual music to concerts at home and abroad.

Suga on stage during the Agust D tour in April 2023.

J-Hope singing solo in Berlin as part of the Lollapalooza festival in July 2025.

Jin's joint tour of the *Happy* and *Echo* albums took him all over the world.

Suga – D-Day

In 2023 Suga, as Agust D, set off on an intensive solo world tour with his album *D-Day*, performing for 320,233 fans. The theatrical production with stunning visuals and dramatic backgrounds kicked off on April 26, 2023 and ended with a bang on August 3 at the KSPO Dome in Seoul.

NUMBER OF CONCERTS: 28

LOCATIONS:

 Elmont New York, Newark New Jersey, Rosemont Illinois, Inglewood and Oakland California, USA

Banten, Indonesia

Yokohama, Japan

Nonthaburi, Thailand

Singapore

Seoul, South Korea

J-Hope – Hope On The Stage

At the end of 2024, J-Hope finished his military service and released two solo singles, *Sweet Dreams* and *Mona Lisa*. Then on February 28, 2025 he embarked on his Hope On The Stage tour featuring his debut solo album *Jack In The Box* and *Hope On The Street Vol 1* EP. He concluded a very successful tour at the Goyang Stadium in South Korea in front of more than 50,000 loyal fans on June 14.

NUMBER OF CONCERTS: 33

LOCATIONS:

 Seoul, South Korea

Brooklyn New York, Rosemont Illinois, San Antonio Texas, Oakland and Los Angeles California, USA

Mexico City

Pasay City, Philippines

Saitama and Osaka Japan

Singapore

Jakarta, Indonesia

 Pak Kret, Thailand

Macau, China

Taoyuan, Taiwan

Jin – #RunSeokin Ep. Tour

Jin finished his military service in June 2024, ahead of the other group members and immediately released his first studio album *Happy*. He followed this up with a second album, *Echo*, in May 2025 so his solo tour covered both albums. He travelled between June 28 and August 10 and visited two European venues as well as the US.

NUMBER OF CONCERTS: 18

LOCATIONS:

 Goyang, South Korea

Chiba and Osaka, Japan

Anaheim California, Dallas Texas, Tampa Florida and Newark New Jersey, USA

London, UK

Amsterdam, Netherlands

WIN

$250* TO SPEND ON BTS MERCH OF YOUR CHOICE ON AMAZON

Closing date: March 5, 2026

You could win the chance to spend $250* on Amazon and receive all the BTS products you've always wanted in our exclusive competition.

Our exclusive competition gives you the chance to choose your ultimate BTS collection of merch and be the envy of all your friends!

With Amazon boasting hundreds of BTS products to choose from, you're spoilt for choice. Perhaps you'd like to build up a set of vinyl records, or fill the wardrobe with stylish BTS clothing, or maybe you'd like to have just one more BTS Army bomb? Whatever you'd like to own, our easy-to-enter competition gives you an exclusive chance to own and enjoy the BTS products you've always dreamed of getting your hands on.

We're offering one lucky winner the chance to create their own BTS wishlist on Amazon worth up to $250* (including postage). In other words, you'll have the chance to own the ultimate BTS prize bundle and it won't cost you a penny!

Winning this amazing prize couldn't be easier – all you need to do is scan the QR code with your smartphone (or type the URL into your web browser), fill in your details and you're in with a chance of winning! Should you be lucky enough to be the winner, we will send you a gift card from Amazon in US dollars or your local currency. Prize amount does not include charges including duties or taxes. The closing date for entries is **March 5, 2026**. And while you wait for the competition closing date to arrive, why not start creating your BTS Amazon wish list and dream how it will feel if you're our lucky winner!

This competition is restricted to entrants aged 18 years or over. If you're under 18, a parent or guardian must enter on your behalf, giving their full details. Only one entry per person is permitted. Full terms and conditions can be found at: **https://shop.keypublishing.com/pages/BTS-comp**

Scan with your phone to enter

If you can't use our QR code don't worry, you can still enter by typing the following into your web browser:

https://shop.keypublishing.com/pages/BTS-comp

*Overseas winners will be able to create their own BTS wishlist (including postage) to the equivalent of $250 in their country's currency

BTS: On Screen

A big part of ARMY's relationship with the group is seeing them in action – whether that's off-the-cuff online meet-ups, fly-on-the-wall documentaries or creative storytelling.

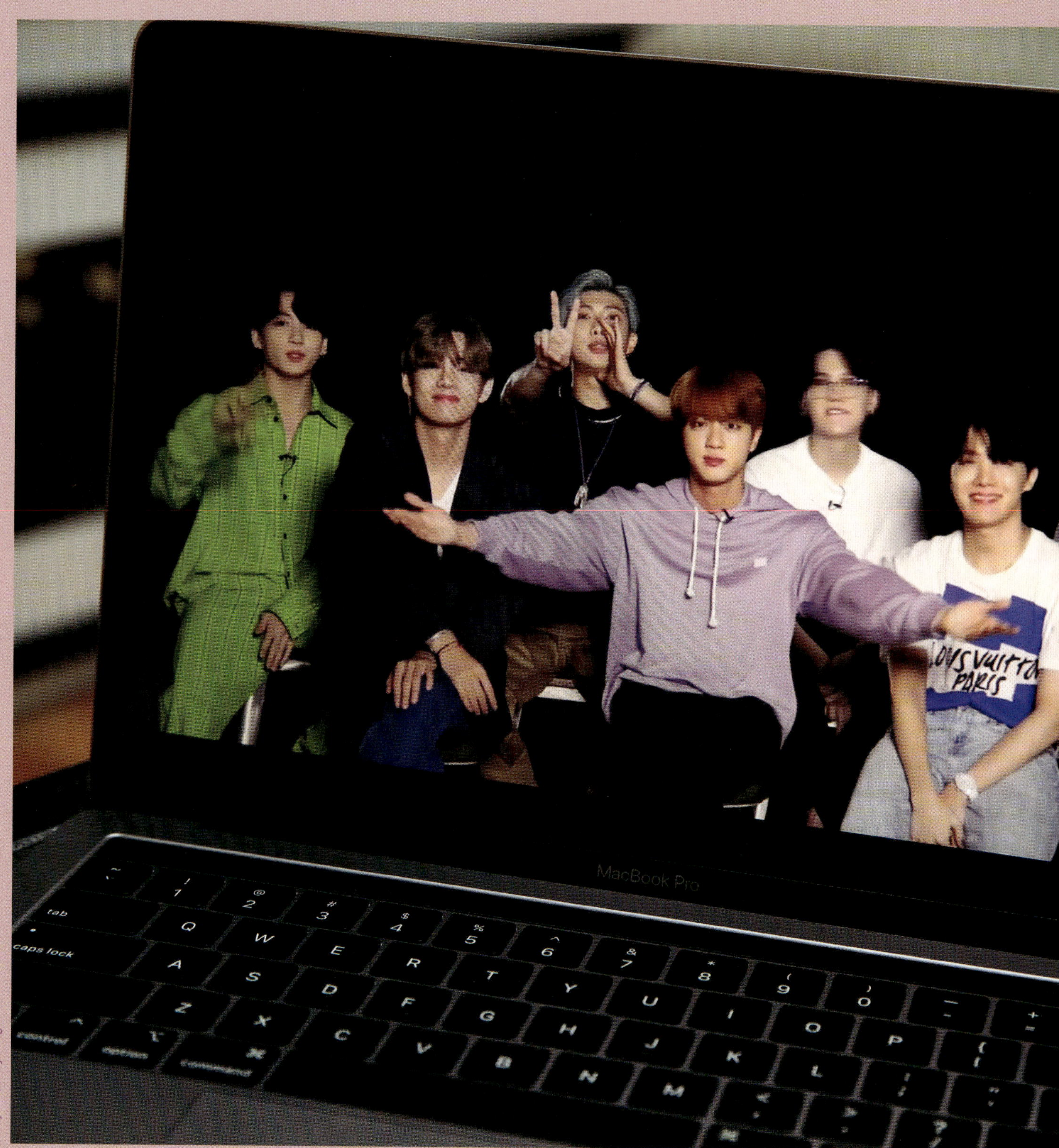

Ron Harvey/Alamy

BJ Warnick/Alamy

Factual Films

BTS: BURN THE STAGE (2018)

This was BTS's first major documentary film, released in 2018. It takes viewers on the group's *Wings* tour and includes exclusive interviews and behind-the-scenes footage. It was the first intimate portrait of BTS as both musicians and young men handling the global fame that had recently come to them.

BTS: LOVE YOURSELF IN SEOUL (2019)

This follow-up concert film documents the *Love Yourself* world tour, featuring performances from Seoul's Olympic stadium. Released in 2019, the film shows the group's connection to the city where their story began and showcases their devoted fans.

BTS: BRING THE SOUL (2019)

The *Love Yourself* tour comes to Europe in this film combining concert footage with scenes of the members reflecting on their own experiences in casual, offstage conversations.

BTS: BREAK THE SILENCE (2020)

The documentary, filmed during the *Love Yourself: Speak Yourself* stadium tour, delves deeper into the personal lives of the BTS members, revealing their hopes, fears, and dynamics as a group. The film has been lauded for its honest depiction of the emotional toll of relentless touring, and the comfort found in ARMY's support.

Online Concerts and Specials

BANG BANG CON: THE LIVE AND MAP OF THE SOUL ON:E (2020)

During the Covid-19 pandemic, BTS streamed this pay-per-view concert that broke records for the most viewers live, to replace the physical tour that had been planned. It took place over two days, with slightly different set lists on each, and was seen by 993,000 people in 191 countries.

BTS: PERMISSION TO DANCE ON STAGE – LA (2022)

Disney+ premiered this concert film on its streaming services worldwide in September 2022, following the group's concerts staged at SoFi Stadium in Los Angeles in late 2021. It features the English language hits *Dynamite*, *Butter*, and *Permission to Dance*.

BTS MONUMENTS: BEYOND THE STAR (2023-2024)

A Disney+ eight-part mini-series tracing the story of the band from their early days to the beginning of their military service.

The Chosunilbo JNS/Getty Images

TV Shows and Web Series

RUN BTS (FROM 2015)

One of the most-loved BTS web projects, this variety show features the boys engaging in games, challenges and tongue-in-cheek missions with prizes and punishments. Episodes range from cooking competitions to athletic challenges, and reveal sides to the BTS members not seen in their other appearances. First available on South Korean streaming service V Live, then transferred to Weverse when the companies merged. All episodes now on the BTS YouTube channel, Bangtan TV.

RUN JIN (2024-2025)

After completing his military service Jin launched his own spin-off web series of the original variety show. Available on Weverse and Bangtan TV.

EAT JIN (2015-2020)

Occasional series on Weverse where Jin eats a different type of food in each episode, and sometimes plays background music and answers ARMY questions.

BTS GAYO (2015 AND 2017)

This was a 15-episode variety web series that could be watched for free on V Live. The boys played music-related games and quizzed each other on their discography, K-pop history, and pop culture.

BTS IN THE SOOP (2020 AND 2021)

The series followed BTS as they took a break from their busy lives to spend some quiet, quality time in a villa complex and then a two-storey house in a forest (soop in Korean) where they could pursue some of their hobbies. These were broadcast on the South Korean pay TV channel JTBC and online on Weverse.

BTS BON VOYAGE (2016-2020)

This was a travel reality series broadcast on V Live and Weverse that followed BTS as they explored destinations around the world, including Norway, Sweden, Hawaii and New Zealand. Each season featured new challenges, memorable encounters and lots of laughter.

BTS MEMORIES OF... (2014-2021)

Compilation DVDs of the work in each year with deep dives into the BTS creative process, behind-the-scenes footage, commentary and personal interviews.

KIAN'S BIZARRE B&B (2025)

A Netflix series that recruited Jin as a staff member on a very peculiar floating guesthouse, looking after tourists and getting very messy. The series, which has been commissioned for a second season, also starred writer/actor Kian84 and actress/entertainer Ji Ye-eun.

Being filmed for *The Late Late Show with James Corden* in Los Angeles in 2021.

" **They make me wish I had such a close group of friends with which to do all types of silly things. Some jokes are hard to get if you are not Korean, but you will feel like laughing with them anyway.** "
Review of *Run BTS* on imdb.com

Solo Documentaries

J-HOPE IN THE BOX (2023)

The process of creating and then releasing J-Hope's first solo album, *Jack In The Box*, and his performances at the Lollapalooza festival in Chicago, USA. Includes guest appearances primarily by Jimin but also the rest of the BTS bandmates. Available on Disney+ and Weverse.

SUGA: ROAD TO D-DAY (2023)

The story of Suga gathering inspiration for his first solo album from some of his musical heroes and then recording his new songs as his alterego Agust D. Available on Disney+ and Weverse.

JIMIN'S PRODUCTION DIARY (2023)

Four videos available from Weverse showing the process of Jimin making music, his relationship with his production team, a quiz show and a commentary on his work.

RM: RIGHT PEOPLE, WRONG PLACE (2024)

The highs and lows in the life of the BTS leader as he writes his second solo album and then debuts it at the Busan International Film Festival.

There was a huge crowd of ARMY and press corps waiting to greet the BTS members as they left their barracks for the last time.

Serving Their Country

In South Korea young men between the ages of 18 and 28 are obliged to undertake military service so that they are trained if the country goes to war.

Korean men do not have to go into military service as soon as they turn 18, they can choose to defer it for a year or more, but they have to start by the time they're 28. However, in 2020, Korean law was amended so that 'artists with merit' could defer until their 30th birthdays.

Exemptions are normally only possible on health grounds, although people who are considered to have 'exceptional skills' can avoid full duty if they do four weeks of basic military training. These have included top athletes, classical musicians and ballet stars.

There was pressure after the Covid-19 pandemic to allow BTS members to request a similar arrangement. In October 2018 they had been awarded the Hwagwan (Flower Crown) Order of Cultural Merit by the government, which acknowledged that they had enhanced South Korea's cultural influence worldwide. Surely that counted as 'exceptional skills' argued their fans?

The Bangtan Boys had other ideas, though, and in 2022 Big Hit Entertainment announced that all seven had decided they would be fulfilling their full military service in the coming months, just like everyone else.

CONTINUING TO WORK

Losing BTS as a group for two-and-a-half years – counting the time between the first member entering service and everyone being discharged – could have had serious effects on incomes and popularity. But it didn't turn out to be the disaster some people predicted, either for the boys, Big Hit or ARMY.

Their music did not fall silent. And

RM and V left military service at the same time, to be greeted by hundreds of fans.

Anthony Wallace/AFP via Getty Images

Han Myung-Gu/Getty Images

Jungkook and Jimin salute ARMY as a thanks for staying loyal while they were away.

"We need to split up once in order to see the value in each other when we come together again."
Jimin's last message to ARMY before enlisting

ARMY stayed faithful. Some of the tracks the group had laid down before entering service were released while they were in, which kept up the flow of new material in those years. And the break after Jin and then J-Hope had gone gave the rest of the group the chance to pursue solo projects – writing songs, producing singles and albums and going on tour. Jin and J-Hope had their chance to catch up when they got out and while they were waiting for the others to finish.

For all of them it was an opportunity to spend time away from the public eye, rehearse some new moves and prepare for a brilliant return to the music scene in 2026!

THE INS AND OUTS
The first to take the big step was Jin, the oldest member of the group. He entered service on December 13, 2022 and served for 18 months, emerging back into the civilian world on June 12, 2024.

Next up was J-Hope, who served from April 18, 2023 to October 17, 2024. Suga was in from September 22, 2023 to June 21, 2025. His service was longer than the others because he was given an admin role due to a long-standing shoulder injury from a car accident in 2012. During the pandemic he had surgery and the combination prevented him from fulfilling conventional military physical training and he was deemed unfit for combat.

RM and V began their service almost exactly a year after Jin, entering on December 11, 2023 and coming out on June 10, 2025.

Jimin and Jung Kook served together, joining up on December 12, 2023 and leaving on June 11, 2025. Suga's release 10 days later reunited the boys at last.

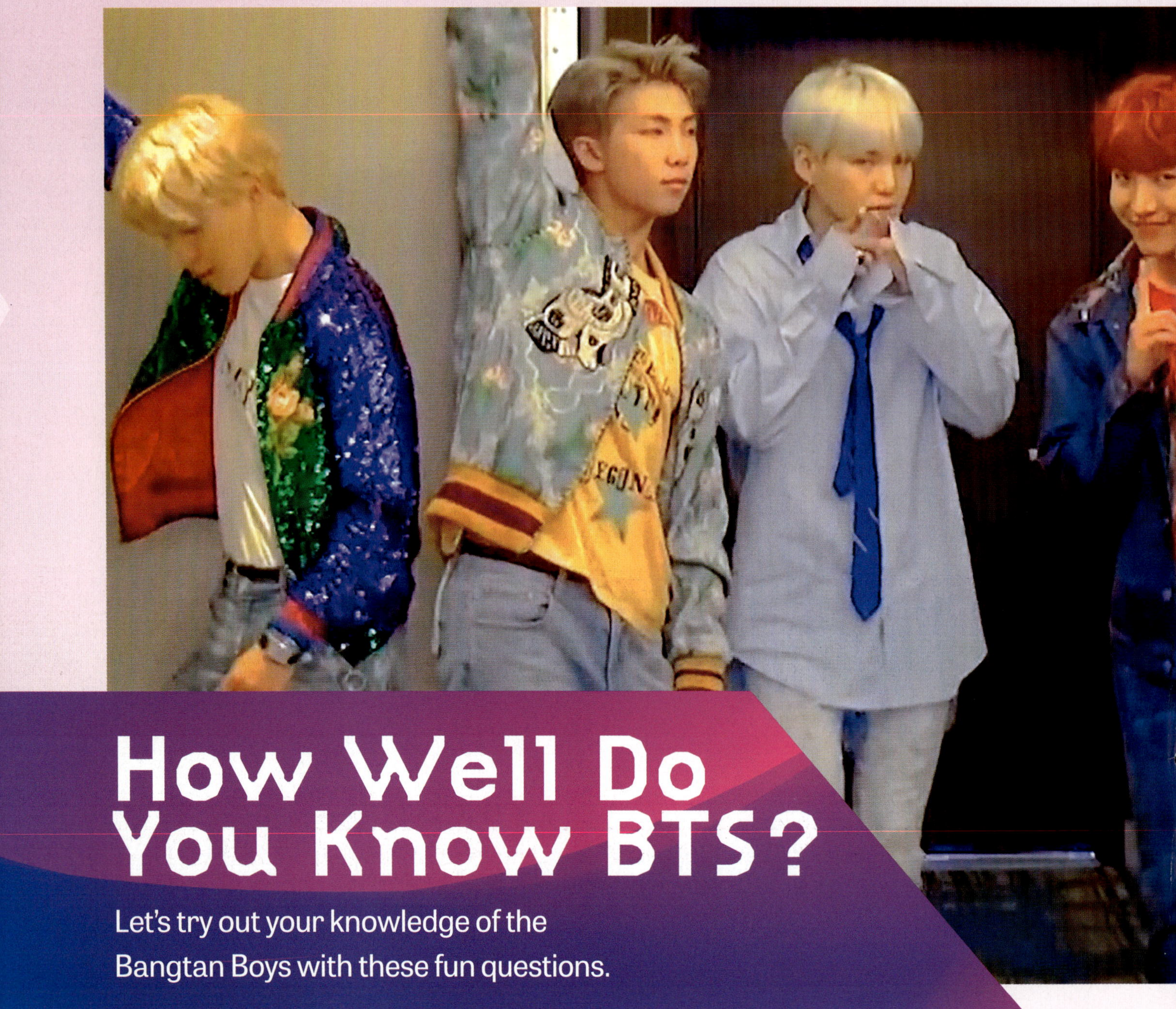

How Well Do You Know BTS?

Let's try out your knowledge of the
Bangtan Boys with these fun questions.

1

What age was RM when he was taken on as a trainee by Big Hit Entertainment?

2

What does the nickname Maknae mean?

3

Where is V's BTS 7 tattoo?

4

Who goes to sleep whenever he gets the chance?

5

What did Jin used to do with his father?

6

Whose sister is a model and influencer?

7

Why is Jimin's nickname Mo-chi?

8

Why did the Korean government give the boys the Hwagwan Order of Cultural Merit?

9

Who is the tallest member of BTS?

10

In which month are the BTS Festas held every year?

KOREA Dispatch, CC BY 3.0 via Wikimedia Commons

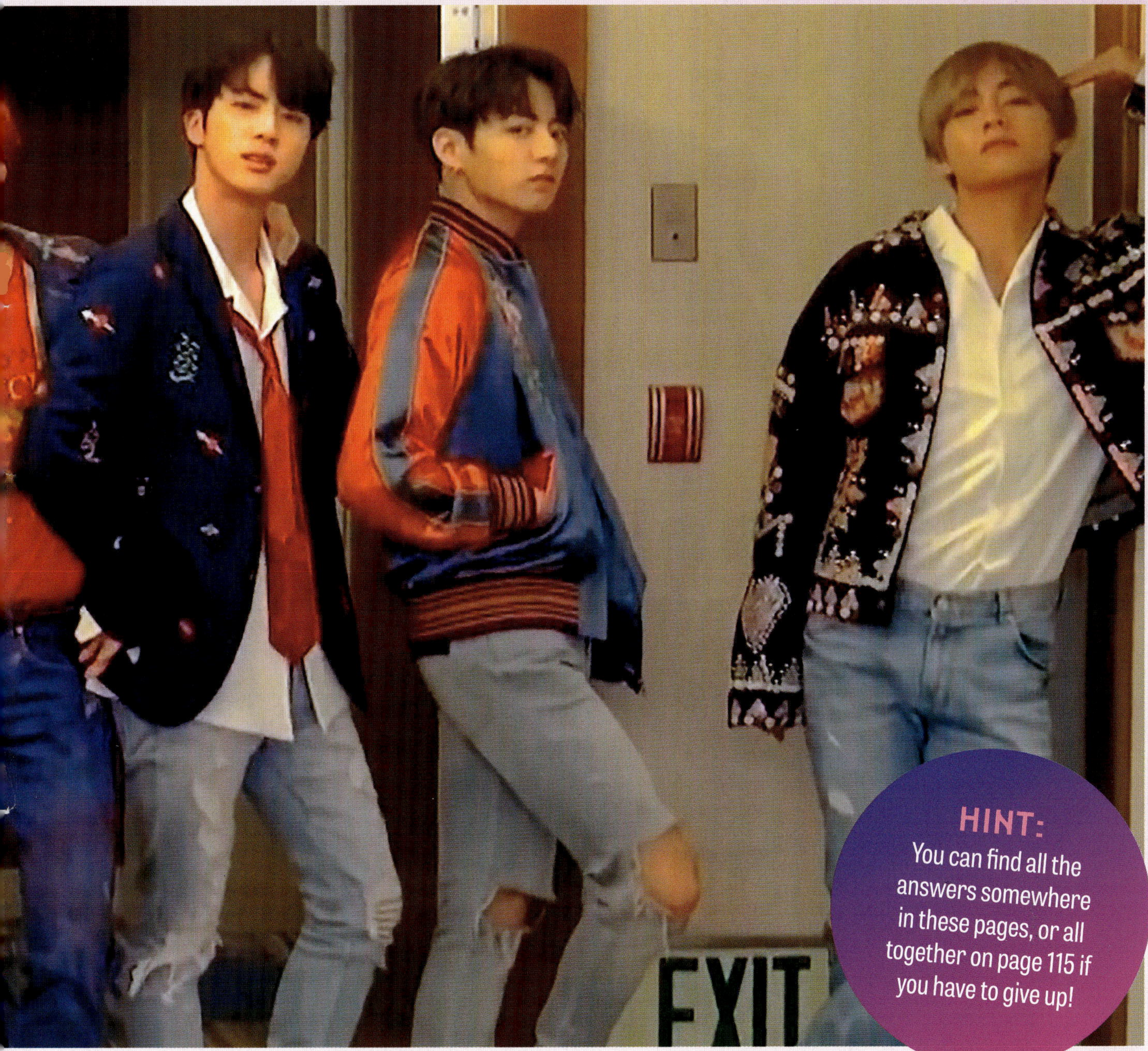

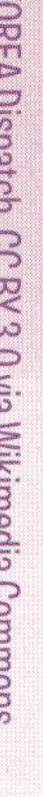

HINT:
You can find all the answers somewhere in these pages, or all together on page 115 if you have to give up!

11
What is the name of the song some ARMYs wrote for the group in 2023?

12
Who created Mang, the BT21 character with a horse's head?

13
Who has a Dobermann dog called Bam?

14
Which was the only BTS tour to visit Canada?

15
How many countries received a live stream of the *Map Of The Soul: ON:E* concert in 2020?

16
What is the tiny heart sign?

17
Which Korean food has a museum dedicated to it in Seoul?

18
Who co-owns a Japanese-style restaurant with his older brother?

19
How did Suga come up with the name for his alter ego Agust D?

20
Who said: "Even if you're not perfect you're a limited edition."

Spanish ARMYs have been lobbying for their country to be included in the upcoming tour.

The offices of Big Hit Entertainment declaring the return of their most successful group.

Looking To The Future

2026 is going to be an exciting year with the announcement of a new BTS album and the first world tour in four years!

The news was livestreamed by the boys on Weverse in July 2025, but when and where will everything be happening? BTS albums have traditionally been launched in spring and autumn and have taken the form of trilogies, with full albums interspersed with mini albums or EPs. World tours have usually taken place around the time of the second instalment in the trilogy. With the break for solo projects and military service, though, things might have to be done differently this time round.

The 2026 tour is rumoured to begin in March, reportedly confirmed by an employee of the HYBE entertainment company that manages BTS affairs. That doesn't give much time for the usual pattern to play out.

POSSIBLE SCENARIO

Mini albums have often been dropped in February and November, so we could get an EP as early as the end of 2025, as a first instalment before the main album comes out.

The full album could then arrive in March, just as the tour begins, which would make sense. And Part Three, if the next venture is to be a trilogy, could come out in August or September, as the boys are making their way round the world in the second half of the tour.

There should be time for this fantasy scenario to play out. From July the Bangtan Boys spent at least a couple of months in the US, reputedly in Los Angeles, working on the musical content of their new work, and we know they work pretty fast and very hard. We also know they will have been working on BTS songs as well as their solo ones while they had their time off from group activities. So laying down the new tracks and creating videos could be quite a speedy operation.

THE MUSIC

BTS issued a joint statement before they left for the States: "Since it will be a group album, it will reflect each member's thoughts and ideas. We're approaching the album with the same mindset we had when we first started."

That teaser seems to suggest that two years away haven't made any difference to what ARMY loves about them. They haven't changed their mission in life. They're making music about loving your true self, acknowledging challenges and hardships in life and knowing they can be overcome, looking after your mental health, and having empathy with other people and a community spirit.

Apart from focussing on familiar themes, there's a likelihood the new album will combine a number of different musical styles - the rock rhythms influencing J-Hope in his solo work, blended with the hint of traditional Korean that Suga has been working on and the ballad sounds of Jin's latest songs. Then there's